THE ELEVENTH HOUR

The Eleventh Hour is a work of fiction. References to real people, events, establishments, organizations, or locales are intended only to provide the sense of authenticity and are use fictitiously. All other characters, all incidents, dialogue are drawn from the author's imagination and are not to be seen as real.

Copyright © 2015-2021 by Ty'Ron W. C. Robinson II. All rights reserved.

Published by Dark Titan Publishing. A division of Dark Titan Entertainment.

Dark Titan Extended is a branch of Dark Titan Entertainment.

First Printing 2021

Hardcover ISBN: 978-1-7366984-9-5

darktitanentertainment.com

WORKS BY TY'RON W. C. ROBINSON II

BOOKS/SHORT STORIES

DARK TITAN UNIVERSE SAGA

MAIN SERIES
Dark Titan Knights
The Resistance Protocol
Tales of the Scattered
Tales of the Numinous
Day of Octagon
Crossbreed
Heaven's Called
The Oranos Imperative

Forthcoming
Underworld
Magicks and Mysticism
The Resistance vs. The Enforcement Order

COLLECTIONS
Dark Titan Omnibus: Volume 1
Dark Titan Omnibus: Volume 2
Dark Titan One-Shot Collection

SPIN-OFFS
In A Glass of Dawn: The Casebook of Travis Vail
Maveth: Bloodsport
The Curse of The Mutant-Thing

Forthcoming
Trail of Vengeance
War of The Thunder Gods
Maveth vs. The Swordman

ONE-SHOTS
Maveth, The Death-Bringer
Mystery of The Mutant-Thing
Shade & Switchblade
Retribution of Cain
The Mythologists

PRODIGIOUS WORLDS
Mark Porter of Argoron (Forthcoming)
Raiders of Vanok (Forthcoming)
Praxus of Lithonia (Forthcoming)

THE HAUNTED CITY SAGA
The Legendary Warslinger: The Haunted City I
Battle of Astolat: A Haunted City Prequel (KOBO Exclusive
Redemption of the Lost: The Haunted City II
Consequences of the Suffering: The Haunted City III (Forthcoming)

SYMBOLUMVENATORES
Symbolum Venatores: The Gabriel Kane Collection
Hod: A Symbolum Venatores Book
Symbolum Venatores: War of The Two Kingdoms
Symbolum Venatores Collection
Symbolum Venatores: Mystery of the Magician (Forthcoming)
Symbolum Venatores: Twilight of the Gods (Forthcoming)

OTHER BOOKS
Lost in Shadows: A Novel
Lost in Shadows: Remastered
Accounts of The Dead Days
The Book of The Elect
The Extended Age Omnibus
Frightened!: The Beginning
EverWar Universe: Knights & Lords
The Horde (Forthcoming)
The Supreme Pursuer: Darkness of the Hunt (Forthcoming)
Massacre in the Dusk (Forthcoming)
Brand New Day: The Dead Days I (Forthcoming)

THE DARK TITAN AUDIO EXPERIENCE PODCAST
Season 1: Introductions
Season 2: In a Glass of Dawn
Season 2.5: Accounts of The Dead Days
Season 3: Battle For Astolat
Season 4: Hallow Sword: Cursed

CHEVAH MYTHOS
THE ELEVENTH HOUR

Written by

Ty'Ron W. C. Robinson II

AND I STOOD UPON THE SAND OF THE SEA AND SAW A BEAST RISE UP OUT OF THE SEA. - REVELATION 13:1

THE ELEVENTH HOUR

We hear the sound of water. Moving quietly as if its still. We hear the sounds of minimum splashing. We know this is:

FADE IN:

EXT. SEA - NIGHT

We see the ocean. Quiet and still. We begin to see the blue sky being consumed by dark clouds that have swooped in over the sea.

> GRAFFOR (O.S.)
> *What we know about the legendary figure known as the Beast is not what we seem to believe.*

The waves begin to pick up as thunder and lightning consume the dark clouds above. The sea shakes as if a massive earthquake had occurred under its depths.

> GRAFFOR (CONT'D)
> *What others believe is the Beast is a simple animal. Lost in the historic times of old.*

Thunder cracks the sky as a tidal wave rises above the sea. The wave crashes into a nearby set of boulders.

> GRAFFOR (CONT'D)
> *Some believe its just a fairy tale to frighten young children to lure them to their beds.*

The water rolls off the boulders, returning to its origin state. Lightning strikes the water. From the depths of the sea, we slightly hear the sound of a horn, mostly like a primal horn.

> GRAFFOR (CONT'D)
> *Some would conclude this theory of mine by asking what are my thoughts about the beast.*

The horn grows more louder as it reaches closer to the top of the sea. The waves bundle as the thunder roars with lighting flashing in the clouds.

                    GRAFFOR (CONT'D)
               I would say, there are things in
               this world. In this universe that
               neither myself or others will ever
               know.

The sea bursts open and the water flies into the air and back
down into the sea. In the midst of it, we see a colossal tail
dive under the ocean with a rumble.

                    GRAFFOR (CONT'D)
               Unless we find it ourselves.

INT. BUILDING - DAY

We see people sitting and walking inside a building as a TV
nearby shows a reporter sitting at a table, speaking about
the news.

                    REPORTER
               We've received multiple witnesses
               suggesting that the civil war that
               has unraveled in the Eastern World
               will soon culminate towards the
               West.

The channel flips to another news station. Where another
reporter sits and talks with a guest.

                    REPORTER (CONT'D)
               So, let me ask you. What do you
               think is causing the rise of
               immorality across the globe?

                    GUEST
               I would assume its of a nature of
               disrespect and having no shame.
               Hardly of anything. I would call
               the term for this, transparency.

The channel flips once more as we see a reporter standing
outside on the coast of the British Columbia, looking out at
the pacific ocean.

                    OUTSIDE REPORTER
               We have no idea as to what is
               causing the earthquakes that have
               been coming out of the Pacific
               Ocean. Scientists and seismologists
               are investigating the
               circumstances.

                                                       CUT TO:

SUBTITLE: LOS ANGELES, CALIFORNIA

EXT. LOS ANGELES, CALIFORNIA - DAY

We see an overview of Los Angeles. We not go to:

                                              CUT TO:

EXT. SEISZONE FACILITY - CONTINUOUS

We're now in the facility known as Seiszone. A division separate from **SCEC, *Southern California Earthquake Center*.** We see both scientist and seismologists going to and fro from one hallway to another. From one office to another. From one lab to another.

Down one hall we see two individuals walking. They are PROFESSOR JOSEPH CROWE (62) and his wife DR. SANDRA CROWE (56). Joseph is the seismologist and marine biologist as Sandra is the scientist and physicist. They walk side by side looking a papers containing seismic activity coming from the Pacific Ocean.

          JOSEPH
You're going to have to tell me more about this because this isn't all accurate.

          SANDRA
The only thing that I can tell you is we're getting a lot of seismic activity coming from all the corners of the Pacific.

          JOSEPH
The Ring of Fire?

          SANDRA
Precisely. We need to look further into it to be sure of what we have that's accurate to what's taking place.

They enter into a lab where others are studying the activity. Joseph walks over to a table where another scientist is standing, looking at the seismic charts.

          JOSEPH
Derek, what do you have here at the moment?

                    DEREK
          We're picking up massive movements
          below the Pacific. No telling if
          its a volcano erupting or something
          else going on.

                    JOSEPH
          According to what we have and what
          I've studied, these earthquakes
          popping up are coming from the
          bottom of the ocean and are getting
          stronger by the hours.

                    SANDRA
          Is there anything else that you've
          discovered?

                    DEREK
          There was something we found on one
          of our deep sea cameras.

They walk over to a nearby desk, where Derek moves onto the
laptop and brings up a video feed of what the underwater
camera had captured.

                    DEREK (CONT'D)
          You have to see this for yourself.
          Its only small glimpse of whatever
          it is.

Joseph and Sandra bend down towards the laptop. On the video
they see nothing but the depths of the sea. Suddenly, they
notice a large shadow swim past the camera, causing it to be
completely dark. The shadow passes the camera and the only
thing that's visible its the end of its tail. Scaly in nature
and as long as a cedar tree.

                    JOSEPH
          When was this taken?

                    DEREK
          Earlier this morning. I'm awaiting
          for the other feeds to come in.

Joseph walks over to the wall, seeing the seismic charts
beginning to go haywire. The other scientist look around and
notice the ground beginning to tremble. Joseph looks around
slowly as Sandra does the same.

                    JOSEPH
          Everybody stop what you're doing
          and prepare for cover!

The tremble grows stronger as it rumbles the entire facility. Joseph and Sandra duck underneath a desk as other scientist run for cover. They know that its an earthquake.

CUT TO:

INT. LIVING ROOM - DAY

On the TV, we see a bulletin saying, *4.0 Earthquake erupts Los Angeles*. We see damage to city, but not critical damage.

                    REPORTER
We have confirm that there were only minor damages to homes, buildings and no casualties have yet to be released.

Inside the living room we see JARROD ROSS (38) and his wife CLAIRE ROSS (30). They're sitting on the couch seeing the aftermath of the earthquake in Los Angeles. We come to discover that the news spread worldwide.

From the corner of the room, we see a young boy walk into the room. He is ELIAS ROSS (7), their son. He walks over to the couch and looks at the TV.

                    ELIAS
What happened there?

                    CLAIRE
They were struck by an earthquake. Fortunately no one was harmed.

                    JARROD
There's grateful for that. Only can tell what would happen if its were stronger.

Jarrod looks over to Elias.

                    JARROD (CONT'D)
Come over here for a second, Elias.

Elias walks over to Jarrod. He picks him up and places him on his lap.

                    ELIAS
You're not leaving again are you, dad?

JARROD
No I'm not. I would only leave if
its was necessary and benefited our
family. I just wanted to tell you
that I love you.

ELIAS
I love you too dad.

The doorbell rings and Claire gets up to answer it. At the
door is the neighbors who live on the same land as Jarrod and
Claire. We see other kids playing out in the yard. Elias
turns and looks, so does Jarrod.

JARROD
Why don't you go play with the
others, OK.

ELIAS
Sure thing.

Jarrod hugs Elias. He watches him go outside and start
playing with the other kids, laughing and cheering.

Claire goes and sits next to Jarrod on the couch. She notices
something is going through his head.

CLAIRE
What's wrong, Jarrod. I can see it
in your face.

JARROD
I'm just getting the feeling that I
will be going back in the military.
I don't know why, but that's the
felling I'm getting.

CLAIRE
You've already done your service.

JARROD
This time it feels as if I have to
go back, it would only be to help
us. Simple as that.

CLAIRE
You cannot beat up yourself over
your feelings. You know this better
than I. When it comes the
conclusion, you will know what's
best for you do to.

JARROD
I know.

EXT. ANCHORAGE INTERNATIONAL AIRPORT - DAY

Snow covers the ground as we see an airplane sitting, passengers are exiting the plane and entering the building. Two of those passengers are DR. SCHEWAZ GRAFFOR and his scientist assistant, DEBORAH PARKS. They walk toward the baggage claim and grab their bags and head out of the airport into a car waiting for them.

EXT. ALASKA OUTPOST - DAY

Graffor and Deborah arrive at a mountain ridge in the outskirts of Anchorage. With them are other scientists as they proceed to enter the ridge.

DEBORAH
What have you found out here?

RIDGE RANGER
We found some fossil that we can't explain. Its best if you see it for yourself.

They follow the Ridge Ranger into the mountain cavern.

INT. MOUNTAIN CAVERN - CONTINUOUS

They entered the mountain and they instantly see a colossal fossil frozen in ice. Graffor is appalled, as is Deborah. He walks closer to the fossil, examine it as much as he can.

DEBORAH
Do you think its him?

GRAFFOR
Not certainly. It wouldn't make any kind of sense if he made it all the way up here.

While circling the fossil, the other scientists light up the entire cavern, Graffor noticed that the fossil contained massive wings and four long horns on its skull.

DEBORAH
Dr. Graffor, do you notice the wings and horns?

GRAFFOR
I see them. This creature is from the ancient times. But, its not the one we're searching for. This fossil is too old to be the one.

Graffor stares at the massive fossil as Deborah watches on. Graffor looks over toward the right of the fossil and notices a trail that goes deeper into the cavern.

                    GRAFFOR (CONT'D)
          There's something over here.
          Appears to be a trail of some kind.

They follow the trail deeper into the cavern. They pull out flashlights to see. While going further, they find a large hole that has been dug out from the cavern and into the frozen ice.

                    GRAFFOR (CONT'D)
          Whatever it was, exited out of this
          spot.

                    DEBORAH
          Something that large moving could
          have caused a small tremor.

Deborah turns over toward the ridge ranger.

                    RIDGE RANGER
          There was a small tremor that
          occurred two weeks ago. We thought
          nothing of it. Nothing could be
          traced by it.

                    GRAFFOR
          Because whatever caused the tremor
          left and it was the source you were
          tracing. We have to find whatever
          did this.

EXT. JARROD'S LAND - DAY

Jarrod is helping other men outside on the land, laying blocks. Claire is in the garden planting with other women as the children play around the garden area.

A car pulls up and out comes Joseph.

                    DOUG
          Jarrod, we have company.

Jarrod looks up and turns. He sees Joseph who waves toward him. He walks toward Joseph.

                    JARROD
          This is a surprise to me. Wouldn't
          expect to see you here.

JOSEPH
Been a while.

JARROD
It really has.

JOSEPH
I am sorry to bother you, Jarrod. I really am. But, I need a moment of your time. Its an urgent matter to discuss.

JARROD
Let's head inside.

Jarrod and Joseph head toward the home. Joseph sees Claire at the garden.

JOSEPH
Its nice to see you too, Claire.

CLAIRE
Same here, Joseph.

INT. JARROD'S HOME - CONTINUOUS

They enter the home and walk towards the dining table. Both sit at the table, looking at one another.

JOSEPH
I see that you're a busy man. Laying blocks and all. I knew you had it in you.

JARROD
I built this house remember.

JOSEPH
I certainly do. I was here to help you at that time. Boy, we surely put in a ton of work.

JARROD
It was needed to get the task done.

JOSEPH
While we can talk about old times a little later. I need to talk with you about joining me on a trip to Miami.

JARROD
Miami? Why would you need me to go along with you to Miami?

JOSEPH
Because you have a historical background of seismology and marine biology. My wife is staying in L.A. While I head out to Miami to discuss matters with the committee about the quake that struck L.A.

JARROD
It was all over the news. Even here.

JOSEPH
They showed the aftermath here? In Vancouver? I hoped that it wouldn't go that far.

JARROD
What do you think caused the quake?

JOSEPH
We're not certain of the matter. Though, what we do know is that whatever caused the quake, started it from the Pacific.

JARROD
So, something in the Pacific had to erupt.

JOSEPH
I want to believe that. But, what we captured on the underwater camera couldn't conclude that fact. What we saw was something I've never encountered in this field. The size and length of the tail was phenomenal.

JARROD
You're saying that some kind of large animal caused the quake?

JOSEPH
I believe it had a hand in it. Though, I am unaware of any kind of animal that size to even cause an earthquake, let alone even exist.

JARROD
What about the Leviathan?

Joseph pauses. He stares at Jarrod. He scoffs.

JOSEPH
I am not buying that.

Joseph turns his head and sees the Ten Commandments on the wall. He turns toward Jarrod.

JOSEPH (CONT'D)
This might by off-topic. But, I just happen to notice the Commandments on the wall here.

JARROD
I placed it there after the house was finished.

JOSEPH
You know how I am about that stuff. I don't see how you manage.

JARROD
Its nothing more than obedience.

JOSEPH
I've said it before. It will take hard evidence and I mean hard evidence to get me to believe in Him or anything related.

JARROD
Which is why I brought up the Leviathan. It could be the beast itself.

Joseph denies. Shaking his head.

JOSEPH
I can understand a volcano erupting underwater to cause an earthquake. What I cannot understand is a beast created by a heavenly entity being the cause. Especially if its some kind of sign for the Last Days.

JARROD
You know I have total respect for others' beliefs. I'm not the one to pressure. But, I'm only suggest the beast. There have been sightings of him.

                    JOSEPH
          I know about the sightings and
          we've even investigated a few of
          them before you decided to run out
          here and stay.

                    JARROD
          Its a peaceful life out here. I
          suggest you do the same.

                    JOSEPH
          I'll think on that. But, anyway I
          need you to come along. Because the
          quakes will get worse and its only
          a matter of time before everything
          on the Pacific gets his by a
          massive earthquake.

Jarrod thinks.

                    JARROD
          Only for your sake, will I go
          along. I go with you to Miami and
          that is all.

                    JOSEPH
          Thank you.

Joseph heads toward the door.

                    JARROD
          Oh, one more thing. The whole
          belief thing. It will come to you
          at the least expected moment.

                    JOSEPH
          I take it that's what happen with
          you.

                    JARROD
          It did. Saved my life in the
          process. Take care.

                    JOSEPH
          You do the same.

Joseph leaves the home as Jarrod stands in the living room.
He looks over at the Commandments and nods.

INT. LAB - NOON

Graffor is standing in a lab with Deborah and other scientists present. They are looking at a board which has photographs of the frozen fossil.

GRAFFOR
What we see here is this particular species is not even listed on our traditional charts of life-forms that have gone on before us.

SCIENTIST
So, what are you proposing to us, Doctor?

GRAFFOR
What I am proposing is this is an ancient species from the past times. One that only a few human beings could ever see.

SCIENTIST 2
This isn't the same beast that you have spoke about before is it?

GRAFFOR
This creature is a different species of animal than the beast that I'm referring to.

DEBORAH
We firmly believe its a possibility that this extinct species may have lived during the days of early human beings.

GRAFFOR
That's what many of you believe. I believe that humans and these extinct creatures lived amongst each other and came across each other's paths.

SCIENTIST
You don understand what's your saying could lead you into a looney bin.

GRAFFOR
If that's the case, make sure the bin has some books and a time watch to monitor.

The scientist giggle as Graffor leaves the board and sits at the long table.

                    GRAFFOR (CONT'D)
          I suggest we not laugh on this
          matter. For this will have great
          effect on the world.

                    SCIENTIST 2
          So, what do you truly believe is
          taking place, Doctor?

                    DEBORAH
          We have one theory that concludes
          to the possibility of global
          warming and the effects of the
          climate change that's taking place.
          The earth is shifting its
          standards.

                    GRAFFOR
          I have another theory to add.

                    SCIENTIST
          What is that theory?

                    GRAFFOR
          I believe that we are in the last
          days of the world we currently
          know. The events taking place are
          an early warning to us to prepare
          ourselves. I can only say that the
          hour of the beast is upon us.

                    SCIENTIST
          Very well, Dr. Graffor. We'll
          examine your work more carefully
          and we'll get back to you.
          Meanwhile, you and Dr. Parks head
          over to Miami where you both can
          speak with the committee about your
          findings.

                    GRAFFOR
          Thank you gentlemen.

Graffor and Deborah exit the lab.

INT. HALLWAY - CONTINUOUS

Graffor and Deborah walk toward the end of the hallway.

>   DEBORAH
>   So, what you told them in the lab.
>   About the hour of the beast, you're
>   going to tell the committee in
>   Miami as well aren't you?
>
>   GRAFFOR
>   There are bigger things taking
>   place and we need everyone to hear
>   it out.

EXT. TOKYO - NIGHT

The streets are crowded by cars. Car horns travel down the streets. The sky is covered by clouds with a little moonlight shining down. People walking on the sidewalks feel a slight rumble coming from the ground. The rumble grows intense as it begins to shake the buildings. People panic and run inside buildings to cover themselves from debris.

INT. RESTAURANT - CONTINUOUS

People pack inside a nearby restaurant and ducks underneath the tables and booths, avoiding the frames of pictures falling off the walls. The rumble stops as thunder begins to sound.

EXT. TOKYO - CONTINUOUS

Rain begins pouring down on Tokyo with thunder and lightning blazing the city. People continue to stay inside the buildings and some inside their cars as the rainfalls.

INT. RESTAURANT - CONTINUOUS

People look outside the windows as they see the rain pouring down. They hear the thunder and see the dim flashes of lightning coming from the sky.

>   CITIZEN
>   Once this storm passes, I guess we
>   can continue on with what we were
>   doing.

The winds begin to pick up and the thunder becomes increasingly louder, though to the people it didn't sound like the usual thunder.

                    CITIZEN 2
          That didn't sound like thunder
          exactly. Did it?

                    FEMALE CITIZEN
               (looking through window)
          Not likely.

The ground shakes again. But it was different than
previously. It shakes again, as if something is moving on the
ground. They hear the thump again and the electricity shuts
off in the restaurant.

People rush over towards the windows as they can hardly see
anything outside due to the increased rainfall. Now, it is
pure darkness outside with the lightning as the only source
of light. The people look outside the window and as the
lightning flashes, they see something moving outside.

It appears to be walking through the streets. Its height is
unbearable to measure from the ground and as lightning
continues to flash, they see more of the object. The lady
looks at lightning flashes and she sees what appears to be a
massive leg that stomps directly in front of the restaurant.

                    FEMALE CITIZEN (CONT'D)
          Oh my God.

The massive object passes by the restaurant and it gives off
a sound of a large horn or trumpet as the electricity turns
back on and the storm calms.

                    CITIZEN
          Did anyone else see what that was
          that just passed by?!

                    FEMALE CITIZEN
          It was huge and unlike anything
          I've ever seen.

Few of the citizens run toward the restaurant exit.

EXT. RESTAURANT - CONTINUOUS

The rain has calmed and there's no sound of thunder or any
sight of lightning. What they see is total destruction on the
streets. Cars flipped over, some flatten into the ground.
They also see some of the nearby building have their corners
chipped off. The female citizen look down the street and
noticed a large crater. She approached it and looked around
it.

CITIZEN
The hell caused this?!

The female citizen glanced up and stared down the street where she saw the colossal object in full detail. She pointed toward it.

FEMALE CITIZEN
That.

The other citizens look and also get a glimpse at the object. It turns a corner, leaving only its large tail for the citizens to see.

EXT. PERU-CHILE TRENCH - SOUTH AMERICA - NIGHT

The sky is clear as we oversee the Peru-Chile trench. We see two men standing on the ground at the coast.

MAN
So, why are we out here exactly and at this time of night?

MAN 2
We're here to study this location. To figure out what is causing these tremors.

The ground slowly rumbles. We notice that an earthquake is taking place at the trench.

MAN
You feel that don't you?!

MAN 2
We're feeling another tremor and this one is strong.

This quake is stronger than the L.A. quake and the ground begins to slowly crack open.

MAN 2 (CONT'D)
The ground is opening!

MAN
We need to go now!

The quake continues to rumble strong, and it suddenly stops. No movement nor motion coming from the ground.

MAN (CONT'D)
Wait. That's it? Its over? That fast?

                    MAN 2
          Appears to be so. Let's go on and
          get out of here.

We see something slowly reach out from the massive crack in the earth. It looks like a large tree trunk.

                    MAN 2 (CONT'D)
          What the hell is that?

It raises itself high in the air and comes down hard. Slamming its end onto the ground on the two men, releasing a loud stomp.

We later hear a loud graveling roar that's coming from the crack in the ground.

INT. JARROD'S HOME - NIGHT

Jarrod and Claire sit at the kitchen table.

                    JARROD
          I need to tell you that I'm going
          with Joseph to Miami for work in
          the morning. I'm going to help him
          study some of the recent
          earthquakes that have been
          happening.

                    CLAIRE
          I fully understand the purpose,
          Jarrod. No reason to discuss it
          with me.

                    JARROD
          I just wanted you to know about it.
          That's all. I shouldn't be gone
          that long. At least a day or two
          and I will be back.

Jarrod gets up from the table and approaches Claire. He kisses and hugs her.

                    JARROD (CONT'D)
          I love you. Just know that.

                    CLAIRE
          I've already known that.

Jarrod smiles. Claire also smiles.

INT. VANCOUVER INTERNATIONAL AIRPORT - MORNING

Jarrod walks through the airport. He goes through the area where Joseph is waiting for him. He walks down the hall and sees Joseph sitting in a chair, waiting. Joseph glances up and sees Jarrod.

                    JOSEPH
You're here. Great.

                    JARROD
What plane are we taking exactly? Because I don't have a ticket.

                    JOSEPH
Neither do I.

                    JARROD
So how are we suppose to go to Miami?

                    JOSEPH
                  (cautious)
Take it easy. We're taking a private plane and we're just waiting on it to arrive, that's all. Should be that long.

Joseph's eyes look over to the right as he sees the plane coming in. He points as Jarrod looks over.

                    JOSEPH (CONT'D)
That's it.

                    JARROD
Great.

They grab their bags and walk outside.

EXT. AIRSTRIP - CONTINUOUS

Jarrod and Joseph approach the private plane as the door comes down and they walk up the stairs.

INT. PRIVATE PLANE - CONTINUOUS

Jarrod and Joseph look around the plane and see it has a lot of room and a number of seats and space.

                    JARROD
Looks nice.

                    JOSEPH
          Yeah. It does.

They place their bags with the chauffeur and sit down in the
leather seats.

                    JARROD
          We're going straight to Miami
          right? No stops?

                    JOSEPH
          Straightway to Miami. No stops at
          all.

As the plane door closes, two men step into the plane wearing
suits. Jarrod and Joseph stare at them as they both sit in
front of them.

The plane door is closed and the plane is preparing for take
off.

                    JOSEPH (CONT'D)
          May I ask who the hell are you two
          gentlemen?

                    AGENT 1
          We'll do the questioning here as
          soon as this plane is in the air.

                    JARROD
          What is this?

                    AGENT 2
          Didn't you hear him. The
          questioning will begin once the
          plane is airborne.

EXT. AIRPLANE - CONTINUOUS

The plane goes straight on the airstrip and takes off, slowly
lifting into the air and hovering.

INT. AIRPLANE - CONTINUOUS

Joseph peeks out the window and sees the plane is in the air.
He turns to the agent in front of him and points to the
window.

                    JOSEPH
          Now, may I ask the question?

AGENT 1
We are agents sent from the federal government to give you details on an urgent matter.

JARROD
What kind of matter?

AGENT 2
There was a discovery at the Peru-Chile Trench. A massive crack was created and something came out of the ground. Killed two men that were there.

JOSEPH
Hold on? You're telling me that some large beast came out of the ground?

AGENT 1
That's correct. The officials haven't identified it yet.

AGENT 2
From some descriptions we've received, the beast had legs like a tree trunk and a tail as long as a ceder tree.

JARROD
(quietly)
Behemoth.

Joseph turned toward Jarrod. Distorted.

JOSEPH
Behemoth? What's a behemoth?

JARROD
The Behemoth is described in the Book of Job. The description you just gave fits it perfectly.

JOSEPH
Now I am not buying this.

JARROD
Why not?

JOSEPH
Because I see perfectly where this is all heading towards.

The Agents look at each other. Questioning.

>   AGENT 1
> What are you talking about, Mr.
> Ross?

>   JARROD
> I know people will find it hard to
> believe. The Behemoth is a colossal
> beast that lives on land. It
> travels on land and through land.

>   AGENT 2
> So, you're telling us that this
> beast that appeared in South
> America is the Behemoth of the Holy
> Bible?

>   JARROD
> That's correct, sir.

>   AGENT 1
> We have some minor footage. If you
> don't mind seeing it.

>   JOSEPH
> By all means.

The agents pull out a laptop and place it for Jarrod and Joseph to see. It plays a video, showing the beast in South America walking across the land, heading into a forest.

Joseph chuckles. Jarrod and the Agents look toward him as he laughs.

>   JOSEPH (CONT'D)
> You know, this is great. We now
> have a monster that travels on land
> and we apparently have a monster
> that travels through the oceans.

>   JARROD
> The Leviathan and the Behemoth have
> risen.

>   JOSEPH
> Land and sea.

>   JARROD
> The days are getting closer.

>   JOSEPH
> You keep saying that and yet
> nothing seems to be happening.
>   (MORE)

                    JOSEPH (CONT'D)
          I'll say this again, I'll believe
          it when I see it for myself with my
          own two eyes. Alright.

                    JARROD
          Sure thing.

                    JOSEPH
          The sooner we get to Miami the
          better.

Jarrod nods and looks out the window. Joseph takes a nap, and
the two agents get up and walk towards the back of the plane.

EXT. ATLANTIC OCEAN - DAY

Two fishermen stand on their fishing boat. They scatter the
water with nets as they attempt to capture fish.

                    FISHERMAN 1
          I damn well hope we get some today.
          Yesterday didn't cut it with me.

                    FISHERMAN 2
          You know this takes time. We've
          been doing this for years.

                    FISHERMAN 1
          Yet, how many fish have we caught
          in the past days? How many do you
          remember counting?

The Fisherman reaches over for the sound radar. He picks it
up and places it in the ocean.

                    FISHERMAN 1 (CONT'D)
          I have a theory that it might help
          us accomplish what we're out here
          for.

                    FISHERMAN 2
          Seems like a good plan.

They listen to the sound radar. Not picking up anything from
underneath the ocean.

                    FISHERMAN 1
          Not a damn thing coming down there.

                    FISHERMAN 2
          There has to be something down
          there. Its the ocean we're talking
          about.

> FISHERMAN 1
> Don't start this again. Keep
> listening in.

They continue to listen and they hear a low rumbling coming from underneath the ocean. The Fisherman look at the radar and notice that the sound is coming from far off in the ocean from their location. Concerned.

> FISHERMAN 1 (CONT'D)
> This can't be right. Its coming
> from way over there.

> FISHERMAN 2
> If this is the case, then whatever
> is making this sound must be very
> big.

They hear the water rustling behind them as they turned and witnessed a large tail fly out of the water and dive back underneath with a rumble to follow.

Both fisherman are appalled at the tail's appearance.

> FISHERMAN 1
> What the hell was that?

> FISHERMAN 2
> A big tail. One massive tail.

EXT. MIAMI - DAY

We see a skyline view of downtown Miami, Florida.

INT. MIAMI INTERNATIONAL AIRPORT - CONTINUOUS

Jarrod and Joseph arrive at the airport. Walking through the airport with the luggage.

> JOSEPH
> We've made it. Now we have to find
> our transportation.

They walk towards the exit of the airport.

INT. HOTEL ROOM - DAY

Jarrod places his bags on the floor in the hotel room. He sits at the desk and pulls out his cell phone, calling Claire.

The phone rings. Rings.

INT. JARROD'S HOME - CONTINUOUS

Claire's phone rings as she is over by the living room counter. She hears the phone and walks over towards the table where the phone is laying. She picks up the phone, seeing its Jarrod calling and she answers.

>   CLAIRE
>   Jarrod.
>
>   JARROD
>   *(over phone)*
>   *Hey, Claire.*
>
>   CLAIRE
>   I take it you're in Miami.

INT. HOTEL ROOM - CONTINUOUS

>   JARROD
>   Yeah. I'm sitting in the hotel
>   room. Just waiting for Joseph to
>   get ready so we can have this lab
>   meeting.
>
>   *CLAIRE*
>   *It shouldn't be too long before you*
>   *make your way back home.*
>
>   JARROD
>   I know. Tell Elias I'll be back
>   soon.

INT. JARROD'S HOME - CONTINUOUS

>   CLAIRE
>   I will
>
>   *JARROD*
>   *I love you.*
>
>   CLAIRE
>   I love you too.

INT. HOTEL ROOM - CONTINUOUS

>   JARROD
>   Bye.

                    CLAIRE
            Bye.

Jarrod hangs up the phone and stares at it for a few seconds.

He hears a knock at the door. He gets up to answer it.

He opens the door and its Joseph.

                    JOSEPH
            You ready?

                    JARROD
            Yeah.

                    JOSEPH
            Very well. Let's go.

Jarrod walks out of the hotel room, following Joseph.

INT. MIAMI LAB BUILDING - DAY

Jarrod and Joseph arrive at the lab. The walk down the hall, being led by one of the buildings' officials. They enter a large room with the words "Committee Meeting" on the door.

                    JOSEPH
            This is the spot.

They open the door and see inside the room a large circular table with over a dozen seats, a electronic board, and tools. Inside the room are already scientists as well as Graffor and Deborah.

Graffor stands up to approach Joseph. He extends his hand.

                    GRAFFOR
            I take it you're Dr. Joseph Crowe?
            Correct?

                    JOSEPH
            Correct you are, Dr. Schewaz
            Graffor. I like the name by the
            way. Its different.

                    GRAFFOR
            People tell me that most of the
            time.

They shake hands. Jarrod looks around the room.

Deborah gets up and approaches them both.

                    DEBORAH
          Its good to have you both here, Dr.
          Crowe and Mr. Ross.

                    JARROD
          The pleasure is all ours.

                    JOSEPH
          It certainly is. So, when can we
          get down to important business.

Graffor allows them to sit at the table. Jarrod and Joseph
sit as Graffor sits next to them as Deborah and the other
scientists listen in.

                    GRAFFOR
          The reason the two of you are here
          is because of what we found in
          Alaska and what appeared in South
          America.

                    JOSEPH
          So, you know what that beast in
          South America is?

                    GRAFFOR
          Correct. First off we found a
          fossil of large proportions buried
          deep in Alaska ice. We discovered
          that whatever the fossil was, it
          came from a unknown species that
          once lived on this planet.

                    JARROD
          Did the fossil have any relation to
          the beast in South America?

                    GRAFFOR
          No. The beast in South America is
          completely different. After
          analysis the footage that we
          received. I've come to the
          conclusion that the South America
          beast is an ancient animal that
          comes from a species known as the
          "Chevah" by ancient Hebrews.

                    JOSEPH
          Is there a name for this particular
          beast?

                    GRAFFOR
          Sure. It goes by different names
          across the world.

DEBORAH
Some call it the Colossus or the Behemoth.

GRAFFOR
We prefer to call it Meheooku.

JARROD
What native tongue does that arrive from?

GRAFFOR
Meheooku is a name that the beast was given back in the days of the ancients. The language is lost to us today, yet the names remained.

Joseph turned and looked at the board where the footage of Meheooku was being played. He points.

JOSEPH
Do you know where the Behemoth's locations are currently?

GRAFFOR
We have been tracking it ever since it arose from the earth. From our calculations, Meheooku appears to be traveling east, somewhere underneath the Atlantic Ocean.

JARROD
Its not that far from here.

DEBORAH
Exactly. We were hoping in a way that the beast would appear somewhere along the line of the coast. Which is why we chose this place to have this meeting.

Jarrod turns and looks at Joseph. He looks at Graffor and Deborah.

JARROD
You're saying there's a chance that it could come here? To Miami?

GRAFFOR
That's correct.

                    DEBORAH
          If we can lure the Behemoth some
          way, we can stop it before it does
          anymore damage.

Jarrod falls back in his chair. Joseph looks toward him
before facing Graffor and Deborah.

                    JOSEPH
          You can't be serious about this.
          Aren't you going to tell the people
          of this city about this
          circumstance?

                    GRAFFOR
          We already tried contacting the
          mayor. He didn't respond to our
          warnings.

Jarrod leans against the table with his arms. Staring at
Graffor and Deborah.

                    JARROD
          So, you're going to just let this
          beast come out of the ground and
          kill these people.

Graffor walks over to the window. He points outside.

                    GRAFFOR
          Do you honestly believe that any of
          these people would believe what
          we're in here talking about? This
          information hasn't even gone
          public.

                    DEBORAH
          We kept them in the dark for all
          intents and purposes. No panic
          means no problems domestically and
          globally.

Jarrod holds his head down and rubs his face. Joseph lets out
a low sigh. He crosses his arms.

                    JOSEPH
          This is going to be interesting.

                    GRAFFOR
          Listen to my words, Doctor. We have
          everything prepared for when
          Meheooku arrives. There will be
          casualties.
                         (MORE)

GRAFFOR (CONT'D)
But, they're necessary for protecting the entire planet from this monster.

JOSEPH
While we're here. I'm sure you know what me and my wife's lab in Los Angeles encountered on our underwater camera. The colossal tail that we seen. Biggest tail I've ever witnessed on a camera.

Deborah leans in. Jarrod looks over. Graffor is now intrigued.

GRAFFOR
Please tell us what did you see on the camera?

JOSEPH
We didn't see the whole thing. It was only the tail. A very large massive tail. The animal had to be unlike anything the world knows of today. It looked ancient.

GRAFFOR
Its starting to come together.

JOSEPH
What's coming together?

GRAFFOR
The events taking place. The distress in the nations, the riots, and the desolations. Meheooku is a beast from the earth and I believe that what you saw on the camera is the beast from the sea.

JARROD
You're saying they're tracking down each other?

GRAFFOR
Yes and they will meet somewhere and it won't be very long before they do. If Meheooku makes landfall here, it could mean that the beast from the sea could make its presence known to combat Meheooku.

Jarrod looks at the board.

                    JARROD
          Do you have an estimate on how long
          it will be before the Behemoth
          makes landfall?

                    GRAFFOR
          Based on its quick movement, it
          could make landfall within the next
          three hours. At least.

Joseph stands up from his chair.

                    JOSEPH
          Then we'll have to clear these
          beaches. If its coming out of the
          ocean, we must clear the beaches to
          prevent casualties.

                    GRAFFOR
          Didn't you hear what we said
          earlier, Dr. Crowe. We can't cause
          chaos in the city.

Joseph stares into Graffor's eyes with intensity.

                    JOSEPH
          Fine. While you and your lab
          assistants begin your countdown for
          the beast's entrance, I'm going
          down to those beaches to warn those
          people of the danger they're in.

Joseph walks out of the room. Jarrod looks and follows him.

                    GRAFFOR
          Mr. Ross.

Jarrod stops and looks at Graffor.

                    GRAFFOR (CONT'D)
          Do not cause panic.

                    JARROD
          We'll do what we can.

Jarrod exits the lab.

INT. HALLWAY - CONTINUOUS

Jarrod catches up to Joseph in the hallway.

JOSEPH
We have to warn those people by any means. Can't just leave them there to die.

JARROD
Let's hope they believe us first.

JOSEPH
Best we go talk with the Mayor before we start running around at the beach like loonies.

INT. MIAMI CITY HALL - DAY

Jarrod and Joseph arrive at the City Hall. They enter in and see the Receptionist sitting at the table. Joseph goes forward.

JOSEPH
Excuse me, but we are here to see your Mayor and its very urgent.

RECEPTIONIST
I'm sorry, but he's not here at the moment. He left for a lunch meeting.

JARROD
Where is the lunch meeting taking place? What restaurant?

RECEPTIONIST
I'm sorry sir, I cannot give out that information.

Joseph rubs his face. Jarrod looks onward.

JOSEPH
Lady, its very important that we speak with the Mayor concerning a dire matter that's heading near the city. Now, where is his lunch meeting located?

RECEPTIONIST
Like I said. I cannot give out that information. You'll just have to wait till he gets back.

Joseph turns to Jarrod. Upset

                    JOSEPH
          We can't wait that long.

                    JARROD
          There's some notes on the wall over
          there.

Jarrod looks around at the wall and sees a note posted saying, ***"Mayor Meeting at Silver Palace Chinese Restaurant"***.

Jarrod taps Joseph on his shoulder and points to the note. Joseph sees the note and looks back at the Receptionist.

                    JOSEPH
          Please forgive my temper. We'll
          wait.

                    RECEPTIONIST
          Thank you for your cooperation.

                    JOSEPH
              (pointing)
          No, ma'am. Thank you.

Joseph and Jarrod exit City Hall.

EXT. BEACH - DAY

On the beach in Miami, we see dozens of vehicles parked as their drivers are laying on the sand, men, women, and children. All wearing swimming clothing. Some are barbecuing by their cars as others are surfing the waves.

                    SURFER 1
          Have to catch some waves today.

                    SURFER FRIEND
          Relax, bro. When they come, we'll
          be ready.

INT. CHINESE RESTAURANT - DAY

Jarrod and Joseph enter the Chinese restaurant. They storm through searching for the Mayor. Jarrod looks over towards the left side of the restaurant.

                    JOSEPH
          You see him?

                    JARROD
          I'm afraid I don't.

JOSEPH
Make sure you keep your eyes open.
He's somewhere in this place.

JARROD
Mind if we ask someone?

JOSEPH
Go ahead. I'll keep searching.

Jarrod walks over toward the main counter as Joseph walks through the restaurant.

Jarrod approaches the front counter. The cashier sees him. He smiles.

CASHIER
Is there something you need, sir?

JARROD
Yes. I'm here to ask if you seen where the Mayor is sitting. I need to have a word with him about some important information.

CASHIER
Well, I'm not sure if I can disclose information on him.

JARROD
Are you serious? This is urgent information here.

CASHIER
I'm sorry.

Jarrod looks around.

JOSEPH
(Yelling O.S.)
Jarrod! I found him! Over here!

Jarrod turns around and sees Joseph running toward him. Joseph points toward the back of the restaurant.

JOSEPH (CONT'D)
He's back here. Come on!

Jarrod follows Joseph in his steps. After making some slight turns through aisles and tables, Joseph stops and stares at the Mayor, who is sitting down with other local government officials.

MAYOR
Excuse me, but why are interrupting this meeting?

JOSEPH
We haven't been properly introduced. My name is Joseph Crowe, a seismologist from Los Angeles.

MAYOR
What about him? Assistant?

JARROD
I'm Jarrod Ross, soldier in the Canadian Armed Forces.

MAYOR
Canadian? What's your point of being here on American soil?

JOSEPH
We have some details concerning the coming event that's approaching this city.

MAYOR
You're not speaking about the whole "monster from South America" deal?

JARROD
What else would we be here for. You have to tell your citizens or otherwise it could lead to a disaster.

The Mayor takes a napkin and wipes his mouth.

MAYOR
Listen, both of you. What I do with my city is my business. Whatever decisions I make are my own. I will not cause panic to this city.

JOSEPH
So, you're going to just let this creature come upon the city and kill people?

MAYOR
People die all the time. It will be no different.

JARROD
I would assume a giant monster is
different than warfare.

MAYOR
I wouldn't know the difference, Mr.
Ross. But, you would because you've
been on the battlefield and have
seen many die. Both targets and
innocent.

Joseph leans on the table and stares at the Mayor.

JOSEPH
Continue eating your lunch and in a
few hours, watch as your citizens
and your city are being demolished
by a beast older than our
civilization.

Joseph turns and walks away from the table. Jarrod looks at
Joseph and turns toward the Mayor.

JARROD
Since you won't cooperate, we'll do
your work for you.

Jarrod walks away as the Mayor continues eating and talking
with his fellow workmen.

EXT. CHINESE RESTAURANT - CONTINUOUS

Jarrod exits the restaurant and sees Joseph standing by the
car.

JOSEPH
Looks like no one will help us warn
the people.

JARROD
We have to do it ourselves. Like
old times.

Joseph smiles.

JOSEPH
You're right.

They enter the car and drive from the restaurant.

INT. LAB - AFTERNOON

Graffor is watching the map on the board tracking Meheooku's movements. Deborah walks up and stands next to him.

DEBORAH
Is it near?

GRAFFOR
Very. Seems he moved faster than we anticipated. He's already in the beaches' waters.

Graffor walks over to the table and picks up the phone. He dials a number.

INT. CAR - CONTINUOUS

Joseph and Jarrod are heading toward the beaches. Jarrod's phone rings. He reaches into his pocket to answer it. He looks at the ID.

JARROD
Its Dr. Graffor.

JOSEPH
Answer it. He might have something we can use. Hopefully.

Jarrod answers the phone.

JARROD
Dr. Graffor?

GRAFFOR
Mr. Ross. This is urgent. Meheooku is already at the beach's location.

JARROD
Already?

GRAFFOR
Its submerged underneath the water. Do what you can to get those people off the beach and into safety.

JARROD
I will.

Jarrod hangs up. Joseph turns toward him. Concerned.

JOSEPH
Well?

                    JARROD
          The Behemoth is already here.

                    JOSEPH
          I should drive faster then.

Joseph speeds the car down the street. Running red lights and
stops signs. Nearly causing wrecks.

                    JARROD
          You mind slowing down just a bit?!

                    JOSEPH
          No. Hell no! We need to get to that
          beach and fast!

The car speeds down the streets. Other vehicles honk their
horns in distress and anger.

They see the beach in the distance not far from where they're
sitting.

                    JOSEPH (CONT'D)
          For God's sake, why are there so
          many of them on the damn beach!

                    JARROD
          Are we going to go and talk to all
          of them or are you just going to
          drive the car into the sand?

                    JOSEPH
          I like that idea but I'm not
          risking damaging this car.

Joseph parks the car near the beach as he and Jarrod exit it.
They run down to the sand where they see dozens of people
sitting and laying on the beach. Few of them play volleyball
and some even running laps in the sand. Others are swimming
in the sea.

                    JOSEPH (CONT'D)
          Everyone! I need you all to listen
          to me!

                    JARROD
          Please with respect, listen to this
          man!

The beach goers look at Jarrod and Joseph as if they're two
strange men who wandered into the wrong neighborhood. One
young man approaches Joseph, laughing and pointing at him.

BEACH BOY
Why do you two still have your clothes on? I mean this is a beach and where are your beach clothes?

JARROD
We're not here to swim around with you.

JOSEPH
Listen, I need you and your beach friends to listen to us. Its a very urgent matter.

BEACH BOY
We're not afraid of some urgent matter. We're all having fun out here and you're trying to ruin the fun.

JOSEPH
We're not trying to ruin your fun. We're here to save your lives.

The beach goers make a circle around Jarrod and Joseph. Their faces show a slight sign of disrespect toward them. Joseph nods.

JOSEPH (CONT'D)
This is good. Now, with all of you here you can all listen. You all must evacuate this beach immediately before the disaster takes place.

BEACH GIRL
What disaster?

BEACH MAN
Yeah? What the hell are you talking about?

JOSEPH
You won't believe me, but there is a monster, a beast that's approaching Miami and we need you to leave this area immediately to avoid casualties.

BEACH BOY
Bullshit. These cult fanatics are bluffing. Trying to ruin our fun out here.

JOSEPH
Listen to me, you little shits!
Leave this beach now to save your
lives.

Beach Boy steps up in front of Joseph. Jarrod takes a step forward. Beach Boy glances at Jarrod and smirks.

JARROD
You know what Joseph. Let's just
leave.

JOSEPH
What?!

JARROD
They want their fun. Let them have
their fun and they'll see what
we're trying to tell them.

Jarrod walks away. Joseph regretting the idea does the same as the beach goers begin to yell at them and throw sand at them from behind.

JOSEPH
We tried at least.

Jarrod scoffs.

INT. CAR - CONTINUOUS

As they enter into the car, they can feel the ground beginning to rumble. Joseph looks around.

JOSEPH
Shit.

EXT. BEACH - CONTINUOUS

In the sea, a rumbling sound rises from the water as the beach goers pause and look toward the water. From the ground in a flash the Meheooku jumps out, roaring of its presence. The beach goers run and scream, panicking for their lives as the Meheooku begins to walk and trample unto them as it walks through the beach waters and toward the city.

INT. CAR - CONTINUOUS

Jarrod and Joseph see the Meheooku approaching them as the beach goers run past them and through the streets.

                    JARROD
          They believe now.

                    JOSEPH
          Its too late for that.

Joseph drives away from the location as the Meheooku enters
the city streets, roaring loudly with its tremor-like roar.

EXT. STREETS - CONTINUOUS

Joseph drives down the street as other cars zoom past them in
fear of the Meheooku. Jarrod looks outside of the window
seeing people running for their lives on the sidewalks and
some are even hit by the zooming vehicles trying to escape
Meheooku.

EXT. CAR - CONTINUOUS

Joseph and Jarrod exit the car as they look ahead from afar
as they se Meheooku causing much damage to Miami. They can
even hear the screams of the people still trapped in the
surrounding area.

                    JOSEPH
          What can we possibly do since its
          already here?

                    JARROD
          We can only pray.

                    JOSEPH
          If you suggest so.

EXT. STREETS - CONTINUOUS

The military arrives in the streets with tanks, jeeps and a
few helicopters that fly pass Meheooku in the air. The tanks
are all in a line, ready to fire at Meheooku.

                    COMMANDING GENERAL
          Ready! Fire!

The tanks fire at Meheooku. It roars as the tankfire makes
impact with its body. Though the smoke begins to clear and
Meheooku isn't harmed by the tankfires.

While they try to figure out another option, they, the
people, and even Jarrod and Joseph begin to notice the change
in the clouds. As it was previously a clear blue sky to dark
clouds suddenly covering Miami and its surrounding locations.

Meteorologists appear on the TVs throughout the area, talking about the dark clouds.

                      METEOROLOGIST
            (on TVs)
     We have no idea as to what is
     occurring just outside in the Miami
     skies as these clouds have appeared
     from out of nowhere and are
     covering the city in darkness.

EXT. BEACH - CONTINUOUS

On the other side of the beach, people continue to sit as they notice the dark clouds. A few surfers notice a wave approaching. One surfer grabs his surfboard and runs out in the water toward the wave.

                      SURFER FRIEND
     Where you going man? You see those
     clouds!

                      SURFER 1
     I do, but I also see that wave,
     man. Its an opportunity.

As the surfer runs out into the water, his friend and others on the beach notice a large moving object underneath the wave as they can see its silhouette. The surfer jumps onto his surfboard and begins to surf the wave. He looks out toward the beach and see his friend and others yelling at him. He begins to notice the wave becoming increasingly larger as he sees himself inching higher in the air.

Low sound of thunder begin to roar in the clouds with small flashes of lightning. Everyone leaves the beach. The wave reaches the city as it becomes a tsunami and crashes into the buildings of the city. The surfer also crashed into the building, killed instantly from the impact of the water to building structure.

The entire area is completely covered in dark clouds as it looks to be nightfall during daylight. Lightning blots begin to crash onto the sand of the beach as a large colossal figure walks out of the sea and into the streets of the city. The figure is very tall to the point where people who happen to be on top of the nearby buildings had to look up at its presence and size. People inside the buildings look out of the windows at its large presence. As the figure walks past the buildings, the wind slowly picks up as low thunder rumbles through the clouds and lightning continues to strike down onto the ground.

INT. STREETS - CONTINUOUS

Meheooku continues to destroy the buildings that surround it as the military continues to fire missiles and gunfire toward it. Not causing any effects period. The Meheooku roars as the thunder becomes louder. It gains Meheoouk's attention as it turns around and sees what its facing. The Meheooku jumps up and gets into a defending pose roaring at what's in front of it. In front of it, we see the colossal beast towering over the buildings as lightning bolts strike near its body and onto its body as the wind picks up. We slowly pan up from its feet to its body to its head. The beast stares at Meheooku with anger in its eyes as it releasing a loud primal horn-like roar, causing the wind to blow 30 mph with the lightning and thunder going chaotic.

EXT. CAR - CONTINUOUS

Jarrod and Joseph see the colossal beast staring down Meheooku. Both Jarrod and Joseph are stunned and are silent without words. Joseph points out toward it.

> JOSEPH
> Was that what I believe it to be?

> JARROD
> Its the Leviathan.

EXT. STREETS - CONTINUOUS

The Leviathan and Meheooku stare down each other, preparing to fight. The Meheooku roars and runs toward the Leviathan, tacking the beast in its abdomen. The Leviathan turns and latches onto Meheooku's back, shoving it into the nearest building. Meheooku turns around and is wiped by the Leviathan's tail. The Meheooku falls into the buildings and onto the ground. As it tries to get back up, the Leviathan rams into it with its knees and feet. The Leviathan starts to stomp Meheooku into the ground as it roars in pain.

The military arrives with more tanks and helicopters as they begin firing at the two beasts. The shots gather the attention of both beasts as the Leviathan only roars at the helicopters, knocking them out of the air. As the Leviathan deals with the military, Meheooku digs and dives underground, leaving the area. The Leviathan turns around, seeing the large hole Meheooku dug into, turns back toward the tanks and helicopters and stomps the tanks and swipes the helicopters out of the air as it returns to the sea and dives in the water, vanishing with only its tail popping out of the water and going back underneath in silence.

As the Leviathan vanishes, the clouds disappear and the clear blue day reappears with the sun shining down onto the now devastated streets of Miami.

INT. LAB - NEXT DAY

Jarrod, Joseph sit in the lab with Graffor and Deborah, looking at a monitor showing the battle between the two beasts the night before. Joseph stands up and walks over to the monitor and pauses the frame.

                    JOSEPH
     What in the hell is that?

                    GRAFFOR
     I'm sure, Mr. Ross told you what
     that creature was I expect. If not,
     I will tell you.

                    JOSEPH
     Go ahead.

                    GRAFFOR
     The larger chevah that appeared is
     the Leviathan or as the ancients
     would call it, Otthuilku.

                    JARROD
     Otthuilku. Meaning "The Last Hour"
     right?

                    GRAFFOR
     That's correct. The ancients would
     believe Otthuilku was called out
     whenever it was the end of a
     civilization or era.

Joseph stares at the monitor and sees Otthuilku's tail. Thinking to himself, he remembers seeing the same tail during his research before the first earthquake.

                    JOSEPH
     Wait a second, I've seen this beast
     before. Its tail at least. During
     my research about the earlier
     quakes, our cameras managed to
     capture this large tail and looking
     at it now, the tail belongs to this
     Otthuilku creature.

                    GRAFFOR
          Interesting. We must keep a close
          eye on the two beasts before the
          governments get involved.

                    JOSEPH
          Wait, why would the government be a
          problem in this. The world might
          need their help on something like
          this.

                    DEBORAH
          The United Nations would cause a
          panic across the globe. People
          would riot cities and towns. No
          telling what could happen if they
          make a public announcement.

Jarrod nods.

                    JARROD
          How would you keep it under wraps
          exactly?

Graffor walks over toward Jarrod. He places his hand on his
shoulder. Looking him in the eye.

                    GRAFFOR
          Take down as much evidence as
          possible.

                    JARROD
          You mean by taking down news
          broadcasts, social media
          conversations, and possible video
          leaks.

                    GRAFFOR
          Precisely.

                    JOSEPH
          Wait a second. The government
          already knew about the Behemoth.
          They would already have information
          on this one.

                    DEBORAH
          Dr. Graffor, what should we do?

Graffor pauses. Thinking.

                    GRAFFOR
          We do what must be done for the
          protection of countless citizens.
                    (MORE)

                    GRAFFOR (CONT'D)
          If they make a broadcasting
          statement, chaos will ensure.

Jarrod takes out his cell phone and calls Claire.

INT. JARROD'S HOME - CONTINUOUS

Claire, sitting at the kitchen table hears the cellphone
ringing. She gets up and walks over toward the living room
table and picks up the phone.

                    CLAIRE
          Jarrod, hi.

                    JARROD
            (over phone)
          Nice to hear your voice. How are
          you?

                    CLAIRE
          I'm doing OK and so is Elias. I
          don't know if you're aware but
          they've been showing Miami all over
          the news.

INT. LAB - CONTINUOUS

Jarrod pauses. He glances over toward Joseph and Graffor.
They notice the look in his eyes. Uncertainty.

                    JARROD
          Um, what have they been
          broadcasting over the news feed
          exactly? Are they showing any
          videos or photographs?

INT. JARROD'S HOME - CONTINUOUS

Claire looks over toward the laptop on the kitchen table as
she watches the news feed broadcasting the fight between
Otthuilku and Meheooku in Miami.

                    CLAIRE
          They're showing the two monsters
          fighting in the Miami streets.

INT. LAB - CONTINUOUS

Jarrod rubs his forehead as Joseph and Graffor approach him.

JOSEPH
(*concerned*)
Jarrod, what is it?

JARROD
Claire's telling me they're broadcasting the monsters across the news.

Graffor looks at Deborah at the computer.

GRAFFOR
Deborah, bring up the news feed from across the world. As many as you can find.

DEBORAH
Yes sir.

Deborah begins a thorough search of nearly every news feed that's flowing through the internet. She stumbles across a couple of reports that are broadcasting the battle between the two monsters. Graffor walks over toward the monitor. Staring as he sees the video of the monsters' battle.

GRAFFOR
They're showing this across the world.........

DEBORAH
In nearly every country that has communications available. Dr. Graffor, this has officially spread worldwide.

GRAFFOR
Father, help us.

Jarrod gets back to talking with Claire.

JARROD
Claire, I'm going to have to call you back in a few hours.

CLAIRE
Ok.

JARROD
Love you.

CLAIRE
Love you.

Jarrod hangs up the phone. He sees the monitor. Concerned about the present state of the world.

                    JOSEPH
        Can we shut this all down from
        here?

                    DEBORAH
        At this rate, its too late. The
        news has already reached the major
        cities by now.

                    JARROD
        People will begin to riot the
        streets in mass.

                    GRAFFOR
        All we need now is for the
        government to make a national state
        of emergency.

The news feed goes black. After a moment of silence, the screen flashes back on as it shows the President of the United States standing in the announcement room.

                    GRAFFOR (CONT'D)
        We must prepare ourselves for the
        inevitable outcome of this
        broadcast.

                    PRESIDENT
         (on monitor)
        Fellow Americans, as you have
        already been notified. We have two
        creatures of a giant nature that
        are running freely across the
        globe. The beasts were last seen in
        the streets of Miami, Florida just
        last night. No sightings of the
        creatures have yet been reported
        since last night.

                    JOSEPH
        What are they going to do about
        this?

                    GRAFFOR
        We are about to find out, Mr.
        Crowe.

                    PRESIDENT
                (on TV)
            *I and other world leaders have
            spoken with the United Nations
            about this cause and the main
            course of action is to eliminate
            these creatures immediately. We
            will all send out military to the
            next locations that will be
            reported by witnesses of the
            monsters. We will also send out
            ground troops to investigate
            smaller areas that the beasts might
            appear. I ask my fellow Americans
            to stay calm as this is only for
            not only your good, but the good of
            the world. I end this state of
            emergency by saying, may God bless
            America and may God bless the
            world.*

The broadcast goes black. Silence fills the lab.

                    GRAFFOR
            This won't do any good.

                    JOSEPH
            What are we supposed to do? I have
            a wife back in L.A.

                    DEBORAH
            Me and Dr. Graffor will stay here
            and continue our investigation of
            the chevah's next reappearances.

Graffor steps closer to Jarrod and Joseph.

                    GRAFFOR
            I suggest the two of you return
            home to your wives and keep them
            protected from what is about to
            come.

                    JOSEPH
            What is about to come? The military
            shooting down our own cities and
            people to stop two monsters?

                    JARROD
            They would do it if they were given
            the order. More than likely, that
            will be the order.

                    GRAFFOR
          Go and protect your wives and
          family. You must hurry. I'll have a
          plane at the airport for you.

Jarrod and Graffor shake hands.

                    JARROD
          We really appreciate this, Dr.
          Graffor. Thank you.

                    GRAFFOR
          Any time.

Jarrod walks toward the door. Joseph approaches Graffor and they shake hands.

                    JOSEPH
          Track down those monsters before
          people begin to die in masses.

                    GRAFFOR
          We will. Trust us.

Joseph nods. He and Jarrod leave the lab.

EXT. MIAMI INTERNATIONAL AIRPORT - CONTINUOUS

The airport is covered with panicking civilians and over a dozen police. The National Guard even arrive to maintain order of the airport. Jarrod and Joseph race toward the site for their airplane. bumping into the mass of people covering the floor, Jarrod looks out of the window, he sees their plane waiting.

                    JARROD
          Plane is here.

                    JOSEPH
          Good. Now, let's get the hell out
          of here.

They walk toward their section and are granted entry. They walk down the long hallway, reaching their plane.

INT. AIRPLANE - CONTINUOUS

They enter the airplane. Joseph places his small bag down on a seat as both sit down. Joseph sighs.

                    JARROD
          You good?

                    JOSEPH
          Yeah. Just didn't expect it to be
          this chaotic.

Jarrod's phone suddenly rings. He answers it.

                    JARROD
          Yes. What? But, I need to get home
          to my wife. She- Yes sir, I
          understand.

Jarrod hangs up the phone. Questioning covers Joseph's face.

                    JOSEPH
          What was that?

                    JARROD
          The Canadian Government. I'm been
          signed to the ground troop level.
          Once we enter Los Angeles, we'll
          speak with the Admiral.

                    JOSEPH
          What do you mean we will speak
          with....? I have no military
          background.

                    JARROD
          They also contacted Dr. Graffor and
          Dr. Parks as well. They're sending
          us all to Los Angeles for their
          operation.

Joseph lays back in his seat. He sighs.

                    JOSEPH
          Dammit. Shit.

INT. GRAFFOR'S AIRPLANE - DAY

Graffor and Deborah sit in an airplane heading toward Los
Angeles. Deborah works on her laptop and sees an anomaly
moving. She gets Graffor's attention.

                    DEBORAH
               (pointing at screen)
          Look. Its moving underneath the
          ground in a quick pace.

                    GRAFFOR
               (concerned)
          The Meheooku. Its heading toward
          the San Andreas fault line.

                    DEBORAH
          But, from its current location it
          appears to be heading toward Los
          Angeles.

                    GRAFFOR
          If the Meheooku is heading toward
          Los Angeles, it will bring
          Otthuilku along with it.

EXT. LOS ANGELES, CALIFORNIA - DAY

Jarrod and Joseph exit the airplane as they approach two
military convoy jeeps. A soldier lead them toward the jeeps.
They enter into one as the soldier shuts the door. Sitting in
the front seats are two soldiers.

                    JARROD
          Where are you taking us, soldier?

                    JEEP SOLDIER
          To the base where you will be
          greeted by the Admiral and the
          Colonel.

                    JOSEPH
          Great.

The jeeps pull away from the airport.

EXT. MILITARY BASE - DAY

They arrive at the military base. Jarrod and Joseph walk
inside the base and see Graffor and Deborah already inside.

                    GRAFFOR
          Nice to see you again.

                    JOSEPH
          Why are we here? I need to speak to
          my wife. She must be in town.

                    ADMIRAL MERYL
             (O.S)
          You will speak to her when the time
          becomes available.

They look and see ADMIRAL MERYL standing at the doorway. He
walks over toward them. No sign of emotion appears on his
face.

ADMIRAL MERYL (CONT'D)
Now, we have assembled you all here for a very important purpose. As you know, there are two creatures of ancient origin that have risen and have been seen by many in the world.

GRAFFOR
What do you intend on doing to lure the chevah?

ADMIRAL MERYL
Simple. We're going to lure them into a large open area and annihilate them with one single nuclear blast.

Joseph rubs his hair.

JOSEPH
A nuclear blast.

ADMIRAL MERYL
Correct. What else is capable of destroying those two behemoths.

JARROD
They can't be destroyed by man-made weapons, Admiral.

Admiral Meryl is intrigued. He stares at Jarrod.

ADMIRAL MERYL
So, what can destroy these monsters, Commander Ross?

JARROD
Only He can.

ADMIRAL MERYL
Who? Who is this "He" he's talking about?

GRAFFOR
Yahweh. Or God as he's commonly called in modern society.

ADMIRAL MERYL
You expect us to just accept this and what, do absolutely nothing about these monsters?

JARROD
There will be a way that the
monsters can settle it out without
causing the death of people.

Admiral Meryl looks at Graffor.

ADMIRAL MERYL
Dr. Graffor, how can we deal with
these monsters without using our
man-made technology?

Graffor looks at Admiral Meryl. He turns to Deborah.

GRAFFOR
The Chevah must fight each other in
a duel to the death. When one is
killed by the other, the victor
will once again disappear until its
next appointed time.

Admiral Meryl thinks to himself as he walks up a set of
stairs toward the office area of the base.

ADMIRAL MERYL
We'll give it some time then.
Meanwhile, We'll need you and Dr.
Parks to continue tracking the
beasts. Mr. Crowe, you will assist
us on any possible tremors that
might occur.

JARROD
And what of myself, Admiral?

ADMIRAL MERYL
You already have been told your
duty, Commander. We need you to
lead the ground troops into the
mountain regions.

JARROD
Why the mountain regions, sir?

ADMIRAL MERYL
The beasts could pop up there and
we need to set up a small base
there. You'll lead tomorrow.

JARROD
Yes sir.

Admiral enters the office room. Joseph looks around the base.

JOSEPH
I wasn't expecting all of this to happen.

EXT. MAYON VOLCANO, PHILLIPINES - NIGHT

The ground trembles as a small earthquake begins. The earthquake is strong enough that Mayon Volcano begins to erupt. As magma starts to pour out of the top, a loud shrieking sound is heard from the volcano. The volcano itself starts to shake as a large object falls from the sky into the volcano. The volcano releases a low deep humming sound before its top blows off completely. Leaving the volcano, we see a large figure, similar to a bird flying from the volcano. Its wingspan appears to be larger than a jet and its tail longer than a train. The figure shrieks before vanishes in the clouded sky.

INT. MILITARY BASE - NIGHT

Jarrod looks at a photo of Claire and Elias. He smiles. His phone rings and its Claire.

JARROD
Funny how you called.

CLAIRE
I just wanted to check on you. Where are you?

JARROD
I'm in Los Angeles. I've been called up by the military to lead their ground troops.

CLAIRE
(frightened)
I thought you were finished with your course?

JARROD
I am. But, this involves something bigger.

CLAIRE
It involves the monsters. I understand. I just want you to be careful out there.

JARROD
I will. You have no need to worry about me.

                    CLAIRE
          Please call me when you know for
          certain that you're returning home.

                    JARROD
          I will. Good night.

                    CLAIRE
          Good night.

The call ends. Jarrod lays down on his bed. He looks up at
the ceiling as he shuts his eyes.

DREAM SEQUENCE

EXT. BATTLEFIELD CITY

We see a battlefield covered with debris from buildings. We
also see destroyed cars, military jeeps, tanks, and
helicopters. We turn and see Jarrod in full soldier gear
running down a debris-filled street. He holds an AK-47 in his
hands, ready to fire at any moment. As he runs down the
street, we can hear sounds of thrashing coming from in front
of him down the street. We can also hear sounds of roars and
growling. Jarrod comes to the end of the street. He looks up
as he is staring at Otthuilku and Meheooku fighting each
other.

                    JARROD
          Shit.

Jarrod raises up the AK-47, pointing it toward the two
monsters. Meheooku suddenly falls to the ground, causing a
large wave of dust to hit Jarrod. He covers his face from the
flying dust. He turns to look back and sees himself staring
at the foot of Otthuilku as it lands to his right. He turns
and sees Otthuilku staring down at him. Otthuilku roars at
Jarrod. He covers his ears as he drops the AK-47 on the
street.

INT. BASE, JARROD'S ROOM - CONTINUOUS

Jarrod jumps up from his bed. He realizing it was only a
dream, but could become a reality.

INT. MILITARY BASE - NEXT DAY

Jarrod walks into the office area of the base. Inside the
office are Joseph, Graffor, and Deborah.

The three are looking at the computer screens, showing signs of the two monsters' locations. Jarrod walks up behind them, glancing at the screens. Joseph turns and sees Jarrod.

JOSEPH
How are you feeling?

JARROD
A little jumpy.

Admiral Meryl enters the office.

ADMIRAL MERYL
I hope your jumpy mood won't infect your leadership with our ground troops, Commander.

JARROD
No sir. It won't affect them period.

Admiral Meryl nods. He turns his attention toward Graffor and Deborah.

ADMIRAL MERYL
Dr. Graffor and Dr. Parks, I need you to see what we've just uncovered from our satellites.

Admiral Meryl commands one of the computer members to turn the channel on the monitor. Changing it to a map where an erupted volcano is visible. They notice how the top of the volcano is larger, indicating its explosion had to have caused tremors in the air and ground.

GRAFFOR
Mayon Volcano erupted last night?

DEBORAH
What caused this?

ADMIRAL MERYL
An earthquake caused the eruption of the Mayon Volcano. But, what was recorded on both sound and video is what you need to see.

The computer screen moves toward a sound software. It replays the shrieking sounds from the location. Graffor is baffled.

GRAFFOR
Play that again, please. I need to hear it again.

The computer plays the shrieking sound again. Graffor looks at Deborah.

                    DEBORAH
          Do you know what could have caused that sound, Doctor?

                    GRAFFOR
          Can we see the video footage?

Admiral Meryl nods.

The computer screen switches from audio to video, where the footage shows a large flying creature coming down from the sky and flying up from the volcano back into the sky. Jarrod and Joseph also witness the video footage.

                    JOSEPH
          What the hell is that thing?

Graffor stares at Deborah. Admiral Meryl looks at Graffor, questions in mind.

                    ADMIRAL MERYL
          Doctor, do you know what that is?

Graffor sighs.

                    GRAFFOR
          From what we've gathered over the years, these chevah appearances are beginning to make sense.

                    ADMIRAL MERYL
          What kind of sense are they making here, Doctor? We need to know these things.

                    GRAFFOR
          Meheooku, the Behemoth, first appeared from the ground. Otthuilku, first appeared from the sea, and now this one. It appeared from the sky.

                    JARROD
          The three beasts of Revelation, possibly?

Graffor nods uncertainly.

GRAFFOR
Possible, but wouldn't dwell on it. They could be symbolic of the three beasts of the Book of Revelation.

ADMIRAL MERYL
So, this flying creature, you've seen it in your early research?

GRAFFOR
We have. Some have called it the Zoz, one of God's three beasts besides the Leviathan and Behemoth. I've come to know this flying one as Rajaooku.

JOSEPH
Rajaooku, you say.

ADMIRAL MERYL
This is spectacular. Now, we have three of these monsters out there and we have no idea when either of them will make an appearance.

DEBORAH
There is a way that we can track them, but it will take some time.

Admiral Meryl looks at Graffor. He nods.

ADMIRAL MERYL
Very well. You two know what to do. Dr. Crowe, they'll need your assistance on it as well.

JOSEPH
I fully understand.

Jarrod approaches Admiral Meryl.

ADMIRAL MERYL
Something I can help you with, Commander?

JARROD
When do we head out?

ADMIRAL MERYL
You speak of meeting the ground troops and heading into the mountain region, correct?

                    JARROD
          Yes sir.

Admiral Meryl nods.

                    ADMIRAL MERYL
          In a few hours, you'll be sent to
          our secondary base to greet the
          troops and you'll be on your way
          out to the mountains. Best take
          care of yourself and your troops
          out there.

                    JARROD
          I will, sir.

Admiral Meryl leaves the office. Joseph approaches Jarrod.

                    JOSEPH
          You sure you'll be OK out there?
          Knowing that not only are those two
          monsters on the loose, but, there's
          another one and this one has wings.

                    JARROD
          I'll be fine, Joseph. As long as we
          don't have any mishaps, we'll get
          in and out of the mountains without
          any damage.

Joseph nods.

                    JOSEPH
          Just take care of yourself out
          there.

Jarrod nods and smiles.

INT. BASE, ARMORY - DAY

Jarrod gears up in his uniform and grabs a glock and an AK-47. He stares at it, remembering his dream and nods.

He walks out of the armory and is confronted by COLONEL SMITH, Colonel of the Canadian Armed Forces and second-in-command to Admiral Meryl.

                    JARROD
          I take it you're the Colonel?

                    COLONEL SMITH
          I am. Are you ready to head out?

JARROD
Yes sir.

Colonel Smith nods.

COLONEL SMITH
Let's head out.

Jarrod follows Colonel Smith to the convoy waiting outside of the base. Both enter the convoy. It drives off.

INT. CONVOY JEEP - CONTINUOUS

Jarrod sits facing Colonel Smith inside the convoy.

JARROD
May I ask what is the strategy for the mountain region?

COLONEL SMITH
We felt it best to let you come up with the strategies, Commander. We've heard you're very good at coming up with them.

Jarrod looks out the window, seeing nothing but wilderness.

COLONEL SMITH (CONT'D)
Billions of lives are counting on you across the world, but only millions depend on you in this country.

JARROD
I understand. Though, I am an Israelite before any other nation on this earth.

COLONEL SMITH
Yeah. I've read up on you and how you live. I also heard you and Graffor believe these three monsters are the beasts of Revelation.

JARROD
We believe they are just symbolic of them.

COLONEL SMITH
Looks as if that symbolism has manifested into something that we can all see and hear.

JARROD
People shouldn't be that terrified of the beasts.

COLONEL SMITH
Why would you say that?

JARROD
Because they're only here for a period of time. More than likely to battle it out amongst themselves. Maintaining a balance.

COLONEL SMITH
We will see.

Jarrod smiles. Colonel Smith looks out of the window, seeing the second unit base.

COLONEL SMITH (CONT'D)
We're here.

JARROD
Fair enough.

EXT. SECOND UNIT BASE - CONTINUOUS

The convoy stops as Jarrod and Colonel Smith exit. They approach the base as dozens of ground troops stand outside, weapons in hand, all geared up and ready for the mission. Jarrod nods toward them.

COLONEL SMITH
These are the men you will be leading into the mountains, Commander. Best you speak with them before the mission begins.

Jarrod nods as Colonel Smith walks sway, leaving Jarrod to speak with the surrounding ground troops. One troop approaches him.

MILES HAMPTON
Its an honor to work with you, Commander.

JARROD
(reading name label)
What is your name, Sergeant?

MILES HAMPTON
Sergeant Miles Hampton of the United States Army.
(MORE)

62.

MILES HAMPTON (CONT'D)
I was brought in to assist you in
the mountain mission.

JARROD
Hope we can work together in peace
and save as many lives as possible.

MILES HAMPTON
I agree.

Jarrod begins to greet the other ground troops as they prepare themselves for the mission.

EXT. SECOND UNIT BASE - CONTINUOUS

The ground troops begin to enter the incoming convoy jeeps that are sitting in front of the base. As they walk out of the base, Jarrod walks out last. Behind him comes Miles.

MILES HAMPTON
You ready, Commander?

JARROD
Yeah. How about yourself, Sergeant?

MILES HAMPTON
Let's take out these monsters to
save millions of people.

Miles walks and enters the convoy jeep. Jarrod follows and enters. The jeep door closes and drives off with the other jeeps in a single file line.

INT. MILITARY BASE - DAY

Graffor and Deborah sit at the computer monitors, watching what appears to be the trail of both Otthuilku and Meheooku. Joseph walks into the office and sees what's on screen.

JOSEPH
You've found them?

GRAFFOR
Apparently so. We've managed to
find these trails and they're
leading us right to the chevah.

Admiral Meryl enters. He glances at the monitor.

ADMIRAL MERYL
You've tracked them down I see.

                    GRAFFOR
          Most of their last whereabouts,
          yes.

                    DEBORAH
          We're still following the trail to
          catch the beasts themselves.

                    ADMIRAL MERYL
          Where does the trails show the
          monsters heading?

                    GRAFFOR
          Otthuilku is in the sea, not far
          from the western coast of North
          America. Meheooku on the other hand
          is underneath the United States and
          more than likely will make its
          reappearance in the desert around
          Nevada or Arizona.

                    ADMIRAL MERYL
          I'll contact Colonel Smith and
          immediately tell him about this
          information. That way he can
          contact Commander Ross about their
          mission status.

Admiral Meryl leaves the room. Joseph turns to Graffor as he
eyes begin to lay on the monitor.

                    JOSEPH
          So, you're going by theory or
          statistics of where they'll
          reappear?

                    DEBORAH
          We're not too sure on that subject.

                    GRAFFOR
          It is best that we keep our eyes
          locked on the two. Though, there's
          no sign of Rajaooku.

                    JOSEPH
          You're talking about the flying
          one, correct?

                    GRAFFOR
          Yes.

EXT. PACIFIC OCEAN - DAY

The pacific ocean moves with the wind. The wind suddenly picks up as Rajaooku flies over the ocean. Its winds are near the strength of a Category 2 hurricane. As Rajaooku vanishes in the distance, Otthuilku's tail slowly rises out from the ocean and goes back underneath the sea with a low rumbling sound.

EXT. DESERT ROAD - DAY

The convoy jeeps arrive in a desert field area, in the distance are a set of mountains. From one convoy, Jarrod looks through the window toward the mountains.

INT. CONVOY JEEP - CONTINUOUS

Jarrod sits back in the seat as he looks out of the window. Miles looks around the area. He glances at the mountains.

          MILES HAMPTON
Those are some large mountains. No telling what could be hiding around them.

          JARROD
You said it.

The convoy jeeps stop.

EXT. CONVOY JEEP - CONTINUOUS

Jarrod and Miles exit the jeep as they look toward the mountains. Miles places his helmet on.

          JARROD
I wouldn't be expecting any movement just yet, Sergeant.

          MILES HAMPTON
Better to be fully prepared than to have no preparing.

Jarrod nods.

          JARROD
I agree with that statement.

Jarrod stands center as the ground troops surround him in a circle.

                    JARROD (CONT'D)
          I understand that I will be leading
          you gentlemen in this mission.
          First, our job is to head toward
          those mountains before sunset. That
          way we can have some light on us
          instead of trampling over rocks and
          dirt in the dark. Everyone
          understand?

                    GROUND TROOPS
                       (all)
          YES SIR!

                    JARROD
                  (keeps a straight face)
          Good. Let's move on out.

The ground troops grab their weapons and begin walking up the
hills toward the mountains. Jarrod leads them up the hills
with Miles to his side.

INT. MILITARY BASE - DAY

Graffor and Deborah continue to track down Otthuilku and
Meheooku from their tracks left behind. Joseph sits at the
table behind them, reading the 1611 KJV Bible. He reads the
Book of Revelation.

                    JOSEPH
                  (to himself)
          All coming to pass, huh.

His cell phone rings. He picks it up and it's his
wife. He answers.

                    JOSEPH (CONT'D)
          Honey?!

INT. SEISZONE FACILITY - CONTINUOUS

We see Sandra sitting down at a desk with loads of files that
show earthquake tremors and news articles of the monsters.

                    SANDRA
          Its great to hear your voice again,
          Joseph.

                    JOSEPH
                  (over phone)
          I am happy to speak to you again.
                       (MORE)

JOSEPH (CONT'D)
Listen, I'm in the city, but I'm with the military right now.

SANDRA
The military?

INTERCUT BETWEEN SEIZONE FACILITY AND MILITARY BASE.

JOSEPH
They need my assistance on these catastrophes. You understand it.

SANDRA
I do. Its not the first time they've called you about something like this.

JOSEPH
(smiling)
Those didn't have to do with three giant beasts that were have thought to be only myth.

SANDRA
We've both known throughout our lifetime that there were things that existed that would frighten us and the world if they would appear before us.

JOSEPH
Well, looks like that time has come and its taking shape. People are rioting across the world, seeking food, water, and shelter to avoid the monsters and the military's attacks.

SANDRA
I'll be spending most of my time in here, Joseph. You don't have to worry about me.

JOSEPH
Just as long as you be careful in the city. From what I've heard its near chaos out there.

SANDRA
You can say that. Don's worry about me. Just focus on your work and after this is all done, we can talk amongst ourselves.

A beat.

JOSEPH
Sure. Love you honey.

SANDRA
Love you too.

They both hang up their phones.

INT. MILITARY BASE - CONTINUOUS

Joseph places the phone on the table. He turns and sees Graffor looking at him.

GRAFFOR
I take it that was your wife?

JOSEPH
Yes it was. She's doing fine in the city.

GRAFFOR
You have nothing to fear. IF something were to happen, she would know to get away from the city as far as possible. You don't live in the city limits do you?

JOSEPH
Funny. You sound like Jarrod when you asked that question.

GRAFFOR
Because he lives far out in the country.

JOSEPH
Yeah. He lives off-grid. I don't know if I could achieve something like that. Its not in me exactly.

GRAFFOR
I'm sure in time you'll understand and learn how to accomplish it if its one of your goals in this life. You'll get it done.

Joseph smiles as Graffor returns to Deborah by the monitors. Joseph turned his attention toward the Bible on the table and continued reading from where he left off.

EXT. DESERT ROAD - NEAR SUNSET

As the sun begins to set, Jarrod has lead the ground troops near to the bottom of the mountains. He looks and sees himself standing on top of the hills, seeing the convoy jeeps down below. Miles approaches him.

                    MILES HAMPTON
         Sir, we keep moving?

                    JARROD
         Until we reach the bottom of the
         mountain, we keep moving. We only
         have a little bit of light left.

Miles turns toward the ground troops.

                    MILES HAMPTON
         We keep moving just a little bit
         further toward the mountains.

A low growling sound is heard from the surrounding areas. Jarrod looks around, so do the ground troops and Miles.

                    MILES HAMPTON (CONT'D)
         The hell was that?

                    JARROD
         We might have company by nightfall,
         soldiers. Best you prepare
         yourselves for what might come.

Jarrod walks toward the mountain as the sun sets and the moon rises.

EXT. MOUNTAIN REGION - NIGHT

The night has settled as Jarrod, Miles, and the ground troops have set up base at the bottom of the mountains.

INT. TENT BASE - CONTINUOUS

Inside the tent stands Jarrod with Miles and three other ground troops. They are looking at a map of their current location. Jarrod points to a location on the map.

                    JARROD
         Now, we do this just as follows.
         Three of the ground troops will
         search the western side of the
         mountains and the surrounding
         areas.
                    (MORE)

> JARROD (CONT'D)
> Another pair of three will search the southern side of the mountains and their surrounding areas. The northern side and eastern side will be search by six troops and myself.

Jarrod looks at Miles.

> JARROD (CONT'D)
> Miles, I will need you to be with the northern side team. Lead them as best as possible. We must be careful out here. That growling sound we hear could very well be one of the beasts.

The teams split up into their pairs. They head out to their commanded locations.

EXT. NORTHERN SIDE OF MOUNTAINS - CONTINUOUS

Miles leads the six ground troops around the areas on the northern side of the mountains.

> MILES HAMPTON
> Check over here as well.

> GROUND TROOP 1
> *(through binoculars)*
> What are those lights over there, Sergeant?

Miles takes the binoculars and looks ahead. He sees a pair of homes sitting in a clear field. Lights appear to be on through the homes.

> MILES HAMPTON
> My, my. Looks like we have people living over here.

> GROUND TROOP 1
> Should we contact Commander Ross about it?

> MILES HAMPTON
> Yeah. Tell him about the homes.

> GROUND TROOP 1
> Yes sir.

The Ground Troop pulls out the radio communicator, contacting Jarrod.

EXT. EASTERN SIDE OF MOUNTAINS - CONTINUOUS

Jarrod walks through the eastern area of the mountains with the other ground troops, who are following him. His radio signals. He reaches for it.

>JARROD
>What have you uncovered?

>GROUND TROOP 1
>*(on radio)*
>We've found a set of homes on this side of the mountains. Do you want us to warn the people inside or leave them be.

Jarrod thinks.

>JARROD
>Don't bother them. They shouldn't have to worry about what we're doing out here.

>GROUND TROOP 1
>*(on radio)*
>Understood. Out.

EXT. NORTHERN SIDE OF MOUNTAINS - CONTINUOUS

The Ground Troop places the radio back into his pocket. Miles approaches him.

>MILES HAMPTON
>What did he say about the homes?

>GROUND TROOP 1
>He said its best that we leave them be. Don't want to cause panic.

Miles nods.

>MILES HAMPTON
>OK, troops. Let's continue searching the area for anything that could be connected to the monsters.

As the Miles and the troops continue their mission, above one of the mountains, we see an object moving. Its shrouded in darkness, though appears to be coming down from the mountain. As it comes down the mountain, it gives off a low thumping sound. The sound travels at a low volume.

EXT. DESERT HOME - CONTINUOUS

A man exits out of one of the neighboring homes. He's carrying a two trash bags. He tosses the bags into a larger trash can. He turns to enter his home before looking up toward the mountains. What he sees begins to frighten him.

                    MAN
          The hell is that thing?!

The man sees the object in the moonlight and the object was Meheooku. Meheooku continues to move slowly and quietly around the mountains. The man runs into his home and locks the door.

EXT. EASTERN SIDE OF MOUNTAINS - CONTINUOUS

Jarrod signals the ground troops to search the left side of the mountain areas. He looks around and suddenly hears the thumping sound coming from the northern area of the mountains.

                    JARROD
          What was that?

Jarrod pulls out his radio and contacts Miles.

                    JARROD (CONT'D)
          Miles. Miles, I need you to pick
          up.

EXT. NORTHERN SIDE OF MOUNTAINS - CONTINUOUS

Miles hears Jarrod on the radio. He responds.

                    MILES HAMPTON
          What is it, Commander?

                    JARROD
              (on radio)
          That thumping sound? It came from
          your direction. Can you see what it
          is?

Miles looks around, seeing nothing but the open field, the homes, and the moon.

                    MILES HAMPTON
          Nothing over here, Commander. What
          do you need us to-

The ground troops immediately begin firing their weapons up toward the mountain area. Miles turns around and sees the troops firing at Meheooku, which roars and starts to run toward them.

MILES HAMPTON (CONT'D)
Run, soldiers run!

Miles and the troops run from Meheooku as it chases them down the mountain. Jarrod and the other troops can hear the commotion coming from the area. He runs over to get a closer look.

EXT. EASTERN SIDE OF MOUNTAINS - CONTINUOUS

JARROD
Miles! Miles! What's happening over there?! What's going on?! Answer me?! Over!

Jarrod begins to hear the screams and yelling from the area. He runs quickly toward it.

Jarrod runs as fast as can toward the commotion, many of the troops follow him along.

EXT. OPEN FIELD - CONTINUOUS

He reaches the location, he sees the remaining troops firing at Meheooku as they're near the open field area where the homes are located.

JARROD
The Behemoth. The homes. Dammit!

Jarrod runs down the hill toward the field. The troops follow him.

EXT. OPEN FIELD - CONTINUOUS

Miles and the troops continue to fire at Meheooku. It roars as it tramples onto the troops. Miles runs and decides to hide behind one of the homes.

MILES HAMPTON
Shit! Shit! Shit!!!

Meheooku walks through the area, inching closer toward the homes. Jarrod continues running toward it as do the remaining troops.

                        JARROD
                    (yelling)
                Dammit! Miles, respond immediately!
                Over!

Meheooku reaches the homes. The homeowners hear the noise and walk outside of their homes. They see Meheooku and begin to run, panicking and screaming. Jarrod can hear the screams of the homeowners. It pains him.

                        JARROD (CONT'D)
                No! Dammit!

Meheooku begins to trample and step on the homes and the homeowners in its way. Miles sees Meheooku approaches and begins firing at it.

                        MILES HAMPTON
                    (screaming)
                You son of a bitch!!!

The rifle doesn't do any damage as Meheooku stomps on Miles, killing him. The area becomes silent. Jarrod takes a look through a pair of bushes. He only sees the Meheooku standing over destroyed homes and dead bodies, some crushed and are flat as paper. Jarrod moves from the bushes and Meheooku turns toward their location. Jarrod stops as Meheooku begins walking toward their direction.

                        JARROD
                Soldiers, we have to move back now!
                The Behemoth is on our tail! Move
                it!

Jarrod and the troops run as Meheooku can hear them, it follows behind, running toward them, releasing a loud tremor roar. They continue to run until they reach the front of the mountains.

EXT. MOUNTAIN REGION - CONTINUOUS

Jarrod looks back and sees Meheooku, who raises its front legs and slams them into the ground, causing a miniature earthquake. The mountains begin to shake as the ground gives way, causing a landslide.

                        JARROD
                Landslide!

Jarrod runs as fast as possible with the troops doing the same, trying their hardest to avoid being crushed by the incoming landslide. As they run from the landslide, Meheooku roars and continues trampling its leg into the ground.

                    JARROD (CONT'D)
               We have to keep moving! Just keep
               running, soldiers!

The landslide eventually catches up to the soldiers,
swallowing them up in pairs as Jarrod and the remaining
soldiers reach the road. Jarrod decides to dive into a nearby
ditch as the landslide comes crashing down on the convoy
jeeps and buries them with the remaining troops.

The area is silent with only the sound of crickets being
heard. Meheooku roars and walks away from the area. After
Meheooku leaves, Jarrod crawls up from a small pile of dirt
and rocks from the landslide. He lays down, coughing to catch
his breath. He takes the radio and calls in to the base.
After which he goes unconscious.

EXT. DESERT ROAD - DAY

During the day, the military rescue team arrives at the scene
as they see Jarrod laying on the ground, they check his
pulse, seeing he's still alive. They carry him and place him
inside their jeep. Finding no more survivors, they leave the
desert road, returning to the base.

INT. MILITARY BASE - DAY

Graffor and Deborah begin tracking Rajaooku on the monitor,
catching the flying creature, they spot its next location.

                    GRAFFOR
               Rajaooku is heading toward Los
               Angeles.

Joseph sees the details on the monitor. He becomes terrified.

                    JOSEPH
               This can't be happening.

Admiral Meryl enters the office. Graffor directs him to the
screen. He looks and becomes worried.

                    ADMIRAL MERYL
               How long do we have before it
               reaches the city?

                    DEBORAH
               Three to four hours at best. I'm
               not sure we'll be able to stop it
               in time.

Joseph rubs his head in fear. Admiral, Graffor, and Deborah notice his change in behavior.

> ADMIRAL MERYL
> Professor Crowe. We will have to send military forces down to L.A. in order to deal with the creature.

> JOSEPH
> But, my wife. She's still there. I need to get her out of the city.

> ADMIRAL MERYL
> I'm afraid we can't let you do that. We're closing the city off from the inside and outside.

> JOSEPH
> WHAT?!

> ADMIRAL MERYL
> Until we are fully certain that we can tame this beast, we must lock down the entire city of Los Angeles. I'm sorry for your wife I really am. But, my devotion goes to the country and its citizens before anything else.

> JOSEPH
> (yelling)
> No. No. No. My wife is still in the city!

Admiral stares at Joseph. Concerned for his well-being.

> ADMIRAL MERYL
> I suggest you calm down, Professor Crowe.

> JOSEPH
> Calm down!

Joseph lunges over and punches Admiral in the face. Graffor runs over and grabs Joseph, trying to hold him back from Admiral Meryl.

> DEBORAH
> Dear God.

Admiral wipes his mouth, seeing blood on his hands. He looks at Joseph and smirks. He nods and punches Joseph. Joseph's weight causes both him and Graffor to fall.

Admiral grabs tissue from the nearby table and wipes the blood from his hands and mouth.

> ADMIRAL MERYL
> I will see to it that you'll be locked in one of our quarantine facilities here, Professor.

Admiral exits the room. Deborah walks over to help both Joseph and Graffor back to their feet. Joseph wipes his nose. Graffor is pissed.

> GRAFFOR
> The hell were you thinking, Crowe?!

> JOSEPH
> The hell was I thinking? My wife is now being locked down in the city and they won't send anyone in to get people out period!

Joseph walks out of the room. Graffor holds his head down in shame.

INT. MILITARY BASE - CONTINUOUS

Admiral sits inside his office and contacts the Air Force to arrive at Los Angeles to deal with Rajaooku.

> ADMIRAL MERYL
> *(on phone)*
> We will need some aircraft to deal with this one. The reason is because the damn thing can fly as well. Best we fight fire with fire. Air to air. Thank you.

Admiral hangs up the phone and sits down in his chair, looking outside the window and in the distance, we can see the city of Los Angeles.

INT. HOSPITAL CARE, MILITARY BASE - DAY

Jarrod awakes up and finds himself laying in a hospital bed inside the military base. The doctor approaches him.

> DOCTOR
> Appears that you're all good, Mr. Ross. You didn't have any damage on your body period.

                    JARROD
          Thank you, doctor.

                    DOCTOR
          You are free to leave whenever you
          choose.

Jarrod smiles as the doctor walks away. From the window, he sees a pair of military jets fly past the building. Concerned.

EXT. SKY - DAY

Clouds cover the sky as Rajaooku burst through them, coming from the atmospheric region of the earth. It shrieks as it comes down closer to Lost Angeles.

From the other direction, we see the Air Force flying toward the city and Rajaooku. The leader of the aerial assault is CAPTAIN HOBBS. He pilots the leading jet toward the battle.

                    CAPTAIN HOBBS
          This is the captain. Prepare for
          incoming. I repeat, prepare for
          incoming. Target is straight ahead.

The jets each prepare to face off against Rajaooku.

EXT. LOS ANGELES, CALIFORNIA - CONTINUOUS

Civilians walk the streets as cars drive in downtown Los Angeles. A pair of civilians hear the jets flying above. They look up, seeing the jets. They point toward them. The shriek is heard as they can see the jets facing the incoming Rajaooku.

Civilians begin to run into nearby buildings to avoid aerial debris. Cars speed down the streets causing wrecks in many places.

EXT. SKY - CONTINUOUS

The jets fly toward Rajaooku as they're over the city.

                    CAPTAIN HOBBS
          Prepare to fire at target.

                    JET PILOT 1
          Roger. Preparing to fire at target.

                    JET PILOT 2
          Preparing to fire, roger.

Rajaooku shrieks toward the jets, inching closer toward them. Its wingspan causes a small windstorm on the ground level of the city, tossing cars and small objects through buildings, to and fro through the city.

Captain Hobbs stares at Rajaooku. His hand on the firing trigger.

                    CAPTAIN HOBBS
          Fire.

The jets fire at Rajaooku. The creature twirls in the air going underneath the jets and behind them. The jets turn and decide to chase Rajaooku in the air.

                    CAPTAIN HOBBS (CONT'D)
          Looks like we're going to have to
          chase this bad boy.

INT. MILITARY BASE - CONTINUOUS

Admiral Meryl is seen watching the battle take place from his window inside his office area. He sits calmly, hoping that the Air Force can defeat Rajaooku.

EXT. SKY - CONTINUOUS

The jets chase Rajaooku through the air, diving and flying through the clouds. Rajaooku shrieks as it flies through the clouds and the sky.

                    CAPTAIN HOBBS
          Fire at the beast when you have a
          clear visual.

                    JET PILOT 3
          Roger that.

                    JET PILOT 4
          Will do, roger.

The jets line up as they begin to fire upon Rajaooku. The jets circle Rajaooku and continue firing upon the beast. As they continue to fire on Rajaooku, they can feel a tremor coming from the ground. Rajaooku looks down and sees Meheooku jump up from the ground, destroying buildings in its path. Meheooku jumps up, ramming its body into two of the jets, destroying them at impact. Rajaooku flies toward the other two jets and destroys them.

Leaving only Captain Hobbs in the air as he is stuck between the cross hairs of the flying beast and the ground beast.

                      CAPTAIN HOBBS
            You have got to be shitting me!

Rajaooku opens its mouth and snatches the jet, killing Hobbs in the process before spitting out the jet. The jet falls to the ground, exploding in the downtown streets.

INT. MILITARY BASE - CONTINUOUS

Admiral sits quietly inside his office. He hands his head, holding it in his hands.

In the other area, Graffor, Deborah, and Joseph also witnessed the event and saw the destruction of the Air Force.

EXT. LOS ANGELES, CALIFORNIA - CONTINUOUS

Meheooku stares up toward Rajaooku. The two beasts look upon each other and suddenly nod toward each other. As the two beasts begin to go their separate ways, the clouds start to get darker and cover the city. Thunder starts to rumble as lightning begins falling from the sky. The sea suddenly rumbles. Meheooku gets into a defense stance, it knows what is taking place. Rajaooku stayed hovering in the air, staring at the sea. The sea bursts open and Otthuilku appears before the two beasts. The three beasts, all in one location at the same time.

The news media flies a helicopter around the location, catching the three beasts on camera and are broadcasting it through the world.

                    HELICOPTER REPORTER
            We can see each of the three
            creatures in awe in the city of Los
            Angeles. We do not know what to
            expect from this confrontation.

INT. HOSPITAL CARE, MILITARY BASE - CONTINUOUS

Jarrod, now dressed in his casual clothing, looks at the nearest TV and sees the broadcast of the three monsters. Startled at the presence of the three.

                      JARROD
            Its happening.

INT. MILITARY BASE - CONTINUOUS

Graffor, Deborah, and Joseph also watch the broadcast on the monitor inside the base.

JOSEPH
Goddammit!

GRAFFOR
This won't go well. For any of them. Man or chevah.

DEBORAH
Are they going to fight each other?

GRAFFOR
We will have to watch.

EXT. LOS ANGELES, CALIFORNIA - CONTINUOUS

Otthuilku roars toward the two beasts. Rajaooku shrieks as it flies toward Otthuilku. Otthuilku raises it tail, going to swipe Rajaooku from the air, but is speared by Meheooku and knocked back down into the sea. Rajaooku shrieks and flies up into the clouds, disappearing. Leaving Meheooku and Otthuilku to battle it out amongst each other.

Meheooku jumps into the sea and starts to trample Otthuilku underneath the water. It continues stomping the Leviathan constantly. Roaring while it stomps. Otthuilku is no longer heard from the sea. As Meheooku roars. Otthuilku rises from the water and grabs Meheooku by its back. Otthuiolku opens its huge jaws and bites onto the neck of Meheooku. Meheooku roars in pain, screaming for its life as Otthuilku has latched onto the neck of Meheooku. Otthuilku holds the body of Meheooku tightly and quickly snaps its neck.

INT. MILITARY BASE - CONTINUOUS

Graffor, Joseph, Deborah, and Admiral Meryl are caught in silence as they witnessed Otthuilku snap Meheooku's neck.

JOSEPH
Holy shit.

INT. HOSPITAL CARE, MILITARY BASE - CONTINUOUS

Jarrod sees the event on the TV. Lost for words. He can only stare and watch the screen.

EXT. LOS ANGELES, CALIFORNIA - CONTINUOUS

Otthuilku hods the dead body of Meheooku and pulls the head with its jaws, tearing the head of Meheooku from its body. The body falls into the sea and sinks down underneath. Otthuilku crushes the head in its mouth before letting it fall into the sea, sinking along with the body. Otthuilku roars in victory and turns back toward the sea, going under and leaves.

INT. MILITARY BASE - CONTINUOUS

Admiral approaches Graffor and Deborah. Pointing at the monitor.

                    ADMIRAL MERYL
        What did we just witness?! That sea
        beast killed the ground one?!

                    GRAFFOR
        Otthuilku is maintaining a balance,
        but is also signaling a greater
        event that is yet to come.

                    DEBORAH
        Do you believe that its going after
        the Rajaooku?

                    GRAFFOR
        I believe it is. We must keep a
        closer eye on the two.

                    DEBORAH
        Will do.

Admiral turns to leave, but sees Joseph sitting at the table.

                    JOSEPH
        Appears that monster did your job
        for you and even saved the damn
        city.

                    ADMIRAL MERYL
        Is that all you've got to say?

Joseph thinks. Making Admiral wait impatiently.

                    JOSEPH
        Yeah. My wife wasn't in the city to
        begin with. She left last night to
        avoid any further events.

                    ADMIRAL MERYL
               Your wife must have a great
               precaution procedure.

Admiral shakes his head as he walks out of the room. A smile appears on Joseph's face.

INT. HOSPITAL CARE, MILITARY BASE - CONTINUOUS

Jarrod walks toward the exit of the hospital area. Seeing troops surrounding the base with doctors walking back and forth.

He walks over toward the counter.

                    NURSE RECEPTIONIST
               What can I help you with, sir?

                    JARROD
               I need a ride to the base of
               Admiral Meryl.

                    NURSE RECEPTIONIST
               Just wait one second.

                    JARROD
               Sure.

EXT. LOS ANGELES, CALIFORNIA - CONTINUOUS

Fire trucks arrive to put out the fires through many buildings. Police are also on the scene directing the traffic that is coming through the area. They block off the entire location of where the battle took place, next to the bay. Other military vehicles arrive, picking up the debris of the crashed military jets.

INT. MILITARY BASE - CONTINUOUS

Admiral Meryl walks into the room, seeing Graffor and Deborah looking at a map of the pacific ocean.

                    ADMIRAL MERYL
               What's going on, Doctor?

                    GRAFFOR
               Otthuilku and Rajaooku are setting
               course for the upper pacific.
                         (MORE)

                    GRAFFOR (CONT'D)
          From what we can decipher and
          indicate, the two chevah are going
          to collide with one another around
          the city of Vancouver.

Joseph overhears the conversation.

                    JOSEPH
          Wait, as in Vancouver, Canada?

                    GRAFFOR
          Correct.

                    ADMIRAL MERYL
          Doesn't Commander Jarrod have
          family in the Vancouver area?

                    JOSEPH
          Jarrod doesn't exactly live in the
          Vancouver area. He lives in the
          outskirts of the city. Far out
          there, off-grid.

                    ADMIRAL MERYL
               (smirks)
          He's a smart individual.

                    JOSEPH
          Of course he is.

Admiral leans in close to Joseph at the table.

                    ADMIRAL MERYL
          I would like to offer my apology
          for the way I acted when the topic
          of your wife was brought up.

                    JOSEPH
               (pointing)
          You're apologizing? To me?

                    ADMIRAL MERYL
          There's no need for the two of us
          to continue budding heads any more.
          We have bigger issues to deal with.
          Like how are we going to deal with
          those two monsters as they're
          heading toward another country and
          why are they leading one another
          the way towards.

                    GRAFFOR
          They're leading one another as a
          sign of warfare.
                         (MORE)

                    GRAFFOR (CONT'D)
          Otthuilku killed Meheooku and that
          might have been a test to see which
          of the chevah would face off
          against Rajaooku. Otthuilku, of
          course won the fight. Now, it
          travels toward Rajaooku to kill it.

                    ADMIRAL MERYL
          So, what happens after one kills
          the other?

                    GRAFFOR
          The victor will more than likely
          return to its previous state. Out
          of the sight of humanity and back
          into history.

                    ADMIRAL MERYL
          Hopefully your right about this and
          the winning monster does return to
          the history books.

Admiral leaves the room. Joseph walks over to Graffor.

                    JOSEPH
          When you said "history", you meant
          something else. What was it?

Graffor points at the table where Joseph was sitting. He's pointing at the Bible.

                    GRAFFOR
          History. There's your answer.

Joseph turns toward the table. A beat.

INT. JARROD'S HOME - DAY

Claire walks from the bedroom and into the kitchen. The laptop on the table flashes the major news report. She sits and sees the news warning citizens of Vancouver to evacuate as soon as possible.

                    NEWS REPORTER
                (on laptop)
          They recommend anybody living in
          the city limits or the city of
          Vancouver must evacuate as soon as
          possible. The reason is for the
          potential arrives of two of the
          monsters that have been sighted
          from Miami to Los Angeles.

                    CLAIRE
          Those people.

Elias walks into the kitchen from his bedroom. He sees the
news report on the laptop.

                    ELIAS
          What's going on, mommy?

                    CLAIRE
          Appears that there will be monsters
          coming into the city. Don't worry
          about it.

EXT. PACIFIC OCEAN - DAY

Rajaooku flies over the ocean as its wings cause a windstorm
to occur. Otthuilku bursts out from the ocean, swiping its
tail in the air, trying to hit Rajaooku. The tail misses as
Rajaooku continues to fly further. Otthuilku roars before
diving back into the ocean, swimming toward Rajaooku.

INT. MILITARY BASE - DAY

Jarrod returns to the base, scars on his face show the battle
he was in at the mountains. Joseph greets him first.

                    JOSEPH
          You made it back.

                    JARROD
          I did. What happen to your nose?

                    JOSEPH
          Admiral gave me a shot. Though I'm
          the one to blame because I gave him
          the first shot.

Graffor approaches Jarrod.

                    GRAFFOR
          Did you see the fight between
          Otthuilku and Meheooku?

                    JARROD
          I did. In the hospital. I watched
          it on the TV. Where are Otthuilku
          and Rajaooku heading next? Do you
          know?

Graffor pauses as his eyes glance over to Joseph.

JOSEPH
Vancouver. The two are heading to
Vancouver.

Jarrod nods.

JARROD
I would say its a good thing I
don't live in the city limits. But,
I need to get back home to check on
my wife and son.

Admiral Meryl walks in from behind Jarrod.

ADMIRAL MERYL
You are going to Vancouver,
Commander. We'll need you there,
but your family will need you
first.

JARROD
Thank you, sir.

ADMIRAL MERYL
You've done your service for us the
best way you could.

Jarrod turns to Graffor.

JARROD
I need you to keep me updated with
any information you might come up
with.

ADMIRAL MERYL
That won't be completely necessary.
Because Dr. Schewaz and Dr. Parks
are also going to Vancouver for
some close examining.

JOSEPH
I'm coming along with you, Jarrod.
As soon as I see my wife back home
I'll be ready to travel with you to
Vancouver.

JARROD
(smiles)
I really appreciate that.

JOSEPH
We're friends. What friend wouldn't
aid the other in a time of need.

Jarrod and Joseph hug. Graffor and Deborah begin to pack their research and their belongings. Admiral approaches Graffor.

                    ADMIRAL MERYL
        Do what you can out there, Doctor.

                    GRAFFOR
        I will do my best. So, will Dr.
        Parks.

                    ADMIRAL MERYL
        I am certain of that. Take cars
        both of you.

Admiral walks over to Jarrod.

                    ADMIRAL MERYL (CONT'D)
        I again thank you for your service,
        Commander.

                    JARROD
        I did what was only needed for the
        people.

                    ADMIRAL MERYL
        You did.

Admiral walks out of the room.

INT. JOSEPH'S HOME - MIDDAY

Joseph walks into his home, placing the keys back into his pocket. He looks around.

                    JOSEPH
        Sandra? Are you home?

He hears a sound coming from the bedroom area. He walks back there and Sandra steps in front of him from the closet. Startling each other, they hug and hold each other tightly as if they never wanted its release.

                    JOSEPH (CONT'D)
        You have no idea how happy I am to
        see you right now.

                    SANDRA
        I am the same.

They release from the hug. Looking into each other's eyes.

JOSEPH
I have to tell you this whole event has been nothing but crazy to me.

SANDRA
The part where the monsters showed themselves to the world? Its that part of the event that has you startled.

JOSEPH
The monsters, yes. But, I'm starting to feel a sense that they're something else at play here.

SANDRA
(crossing arms)
What are you talking about?

JOSEPH
Jarrod has always been a spiritual guy from the time we met on the field. Dr. Graffor is a guy I'm not sure on having dinner with because he's so deep into the stuff.

SANDRA
Oh. I'm starting to see where this is all going.

Joseph looks at his wife. Paused for a moment.

JOSEPH
You sure?

SANDRA
The biblical part of it all. I know that your not a complete believer. But, those three monsters did arrive from the locations that were given in Revelation.

JOSEPH
I know. I read the entire Book of Revelation to get its understanding.

SANDRA
You opened the Bible?! That's something new coming from you.

                    JOSEPH
          Don't get all sassy because of it.
          I've never seen you reading the
          thing.

Sandra scoffs.

                    SANDRA
          I've did my part in reading it. It
          has always been you that's had a
          hard time to deal with it.

                    JOSEPH
          You're right about that, of course.

Joseph walks into his bedroom and places his suitcase in the
corner. He starts to grab some clothes from the closet and
begins changing his outfit. Sandra notices him changing his
clothes.

                    SANDRA
          Where are you off to now?

                    JOSEPH
          I'm going with Jarrod to Vancouver.
          Its important that I go.

                    SANDRA
          But, you just got back.

                    JOSEPH
          I know. I know. But, believe me, I
          will come back when all of this
          monster jumbo stuff is over. OK?

                    SANDRA
          OK. I believe you.

They kiss. Joseph leaves the home.

EXT. LAX AIRPORT - MIDDAY

Joseph arrives at the airport by cab. He walks to the
entrance.

INT. LAX AIRPORT - CONTINUOUS

Joseph enters the airport and sees Jarrod ahead. He walks
over toward him.

                    JARROD
          Just in time.

JOSEPH
I had to speak with my wife. She understands the whole deal.

JARROD
That's good. How did she take the monster stuff?

JOSEPH
She seems calm about the whole thing. I'm the one that's going crazy over it. I'm not used to events like these. I'm more used to dealing with tremors and seismic activities. Dealing with monsters that I believed were once fiction, but have been proved to be a reality. It frightens you.

Jarrod listens closely.

JOSEPH (CONT'D)
Things like that begin to open your understanding about the universe.

JARROD
The whole "We're not alone" idea?

JOSEPH
To a point, yes. But, with more of an earthly discovery. There's no telling what else is hidden from us that lives on the same planet with us.

They walk toward the location. Seeing the plane waiting for them on the outside.

EXT - LAX AIRPORT - CONTINUOUS

Their plane sits, waiting on them to enter.

INT. AIRPLANE - CONTINUOUS

Jarrod and Joseph enter the plane. The door closes.

JOSEPH
Do you know if Graffor and Deborah arrived in Vancouver already?

                    JARROD
          They took a plane ride after we
          left the base. I would expect them
          to be reaching Vancouver within an
          hour.

Joseph nods.

                    JOSEPH
          I better get some decent rest
          before we get ready for our final
          course.

Jarrod smiles as Joseph lays back in his seat. Eyes close.
Reaching for his sleep.

INT. MILITARY BASE - MIDDAY

Admiral walks through the headquarters as his soldiers have
received information from Graffor.

                    ADMIRAL MERYL
          Upload the message.

                    SOLDIER
          Yes sir.

They upload the message and its a map, showing the west coast
of Canada and two large objects moving toward Vancouver.
Otthuilku and Rajaooku.

                    ADMIRAL MERYL
          They're closer that we anticipated.
          How long will it be before they
          reach land?

                    SOLDIER
          Judging by this information, the
          monsters will arrive in the city by
          sunset.

Admiral approaches two of the soldiers standing.

                    ADMIRAL MERYL
          Contact your forces and tell them
          we need dozens of military fire to
          be sent to Vancouver immediately.
          Do not take no for an answer. I am
          clear?

                    SOLDIERS
          Yes sir.

The soldiers exit the room. Admiral Meryl stares at the map. Worried about the coming event to take place.

                ADMIRAL MERYL
     May God be with us all on this one.

EXT. AIRPLANE - MIDDAY

Jarrod's phone beeps. He takes it from his pocket and looks. Its a message from Graffor. He opens the message and its the same map sent to Admiral Meryl.

                JARROD
     They're closer.

Joseph overhears Jarrod in his sleep. He moves his head.

                JOSEPH
         (raising up)
     Who's closer?

                JARROD
     What? Oh, the monsters, they're
     closer to Vancouver than what we
     previously thought.

                JOSEPH
     Then, how close are we to
     Vancouver? Will we make it there
     before they do?

                JARROD
         (looks at watch)
     An hour and twenty-five minutes.
     We're not that far from Vancouver.
     We should make it there before they
     do. Otherwise, this plane ride
     would be much more bumper that what
     it is now.

Joseph scoffs. He looks through the window and sees a set of clouds slowly forming around the sky. Grey clouds to be precise.

                JOSEPH
     I think we'll have some kind of
     bumpy ride anyway.

                JARROD
     Why?

Joseph points outside. Jarrod looks and sees the clouds. A possible thunderstorm.

                    JARROD (CONT'D)
          We'll be fine. I'll take a storm
          over the monsters.

                    JOSEPH
          For once in that I agree with you.

They laugh.

EXT. PACIFIC OCEAN, NEAR WEST COAST OF CANADA - DAY

The Navy arrives with battleships. Above them arrives Rajaooku, shrieking loudly. From the sea, Otthuilku appears as the Navy ships begin firing on the two monsters. The weapons do not harm the monsters as they're trying to come to blows with each other. Rajaooku swoops down toward Otthuilku, scratching it with its talons and pecks it in its shoulder with its beak. Otthuilku stumbles before raising its tail up and swiping Rajaooku in the back.

INT. NAVY BATTLESHIP - CONTINUOUS

                    NAVY COMMANDER
          Continue firing your weapons! Fire
          torpedoes!

EXT. PACIFIC OCEAN, NEAR WEST COAST OF CANADA - CONTINUOUS

The battleships begin firing their torpedoes at the monsters. Otthuilku dives underneath the ships as Rajaooku twirls and swoops past the torpedoes.

                    NAVY COMMANDER
          Fire machine guns!

The machine guns fire at the monsters. Rajaooku swoops down toward one of the battleships and tips it over with its beak. Otthuilku rises out of the water and slams its arm into the other battleship, snapping it in half.

INT. NAVY BATTLESHIP - CONTINUOUS

                    NAVY SOLDIER
          What shall we do, sir?

                    NAVY COMMANDER
          We keep firing until either we're
          dead or the beasts are! Keep firing
          at the targets!

The Navy continues to fire at the monsters. Otthuilku begins destroying the surrounding ships while trying to knock Rajaooku out of the sky with its tail. Rajaooku swoops back and forth through the fire, trying to knock over Otthuilku while destroying the ships.

NAVY SOLDIER
Sir, we can't continue like this. We'll run out of ammo and then we're done for.

NAVY COMMANDER
Doesn't matter, soldier. We were given this mission and it is our job to accomplish it. Keep the ships firing.

The soldier sighs before walking away.

EXT. PACIFIC OCEAN, NEAR WEST COAST OF CANADA - CONTINUOUS

Navy aircraft begin to take off and turn around, chasing and firing at Rajaooku in the air as a pair of submarines arrive underneath the water. The submarines fire at the legs of Otthuilku. It roars and slams its tail in the sea, causing an in-sea tsunami that rams into the nearby Navy ship. Otthuilku dives underwater.

EXT. UNDERWATER - CONTINUOUS

Otthuilku swims underwater avoiding the ballistic missiles firing from the submarines. Its tail rams into one of the submarines, knocking it off course and into another submarines as they both crash into the nearby rock and fall to the floor.

SUBMARINE PILOT
Firing more ballistic missiles.

The missiles fire out and run into the large rocks underneath the water. Otthuilku turns around and swims at fast pace directly in front of the submarine.

SUBMARINE PILOT (CONT'D)
The hell is that thing doing? Its coming straight for us!

Otthuilku moves fast as it becomes closer to have a head-on collision with the submarine.

SUBMARINE PILOT (CONT'D)
Brace yourselves, people!

Otthuilku rams head first into the submarine, causing it to explode. Otthuilku swims through the fire and debris of the demolished submarine.

EXT. PACIFIC OCEAN, NEAR WEST COAST OF CANADA - CONTINUOUS

The explosion was felt above the water by the Navy ships.

The aircraft continue firing at Rajaooku, until Rajaooku hovers above them and claws them with its talons in the air. The crafts fall into the water in mass.

Otthuilku bursts from the water, looking up toward Rajaooku as the crafts continue to fall and fall onto Otthuilku. Otthuilku dives back into the water, moving to another location. Rajaooku shrieks and flies off as Otthuilku can be seen underwater swimming behind Rajaooku, following the monster.

                NAVY SOLDIER
    What do we do now, sir?

                NAVY COMMANDER
    We report back to the Admiral. See
    what he wants us to do about these
    monsters.

EXT. VANCOUVER, BRITISH COLUMBIA, CANADA - MIDDAY

The city is in near chaos as traffic holds up the streets and people begin to loot grocery stores and electronic stores.

People in their cars honk their horns to the ones in front. Yelling at them to make a move ahead. Signaling they can't move ahead in their vehicles, some drivers exit their vehicles and start yelling and screaming at the other drivers. Some of the other drivers aren't taking the yelling completely as fights begin to break out in the traffic jammed streets.

Women and children start screaming as they watch the fights take place in horror.

EXT. VANCOUVER AIRPORT - CONTINUOUS

Jarrod and Joseph arrive in Vancouver. Jarrod looks around and sees his car.

                JARROD
    There's my car.

JOSEPH
          After the announcement, you think
          they'll be a long traffic jam?

                    JARROD
          Yeah. Though the thing is I don't
          take the usual roads.

They enter into the car.

The car shuts on.

The car drives off.

EXT. VANCOUVER, BRITISH COLUMBIA, CANADA - CONTINUOUS

The fights continue to take place as more have grown through the amount of time waiting. People have lost their patience and are taking their anger out on the people surrounding them.

One man grabs another and smacks him across the face.

                    MAN
          Why didn't you move your ass ahead!
          Holding the rest of us off, you
          piece of shit!

One mother covers her children's eyes as the watch a woman being dragged out of her car by two men who are trying to have their way with her.

                    WOMAN
          Please, let me go!!!

                    MAN
          I'll let go once I've had my way
          with you, honey!

                    MAN 2
          She's a good looking piece of ass,
          man! I want to go first!

The man rips her shirt. She screams as the other man grabs him and starts pummeling him in his face. After which, he turns back to the woman. Wiping the other man's blood from his knuckles onto the woman's ripped shirt.

                    MAN
          This won't take long, sweetie. Just
          let me do what I want with you and
          I'll be out of your hair.

The man pulls her dress as gunshots start to fire. The man jumps as a few civilians begin firing at each other without any aiming. Just chaotic firing.

As the sun begins to set, a loud shriek comes from the sky. The riots cease as the people begin to look up into the air. Clouds cover the city as even more darker clouds can be seen in the horizon, reaching closer.

Two planes fall from the sky. One falls into the nearby bay as the other one crashes into a building. The people scream in terror as they come to silence.

From the clouds after a moment of silence, Rajaooku bursts through them and begins flying over the city of Vancouver.

Its loud shrieks frighten the people as they try to look for cover. Ones still in their cars begin to ram through the traffic, trying to get out of the way of Rajaooku.

People are ran over by the crazed traffic. Rajaooku continues shrieking as its wings blow wind through the city, tearing up anything that's in the path. Rajaooku continues to shriek, indicating its presence and stance amongst humanity.

Thunder begins to rumble from the dark clouds that have made themselves above the city. Rajaooku looks up at the clouds. Seeing the lightning striking and the rain begins to pour.

Rajaooku looks toward the bay. Seeing the waves beginning to come in. As the waves pour into the bay from the sea, a primal roar is sounded. Rajaooku stands its ground, watching the bay.

From the bay, Otthuilku rises, roaring of its presence, similar to that of the angels' blowing of the trumpets. Lightning strikes in the background behind Otthuilku.

INT. JARROD'S HOME - NIGHT

Claire washes dishes when she hears the door open and in comes Jarrod and Joseph.

          CLAIRE
  Jarrod. You're back.

They hug and kiss. Elias walks out from his room and sees his father. He runs toward him.

          ELIAS
Dad!

JARROD
Hey son.

Jarrod hugs his son. Joseph smiles.

JARROD (CONT'D)
I've missed you so much. How have you behaved since I've been gone?

ELIAS
Good.

JARROD
Good, huh. That's my boy.

Jarrod looks to Joseph.

CLAIRE
Nice to see you again, Joseph.

JOSEPH
Same here, Mrs. Ross.

CLAIRE
Are you here to stay?

JARROD
I am.

Jarrod's phone rings, so does Joseph's. They look at one another before answering their phones.

JARROD (CONT'D)
Its Graffor.

JOSEPH
I have Deborah on this one.

They answer their phones, moving to other sides of the living room.

GRAFFOR
Jarrod, you need to come to the lab. You need to see what is happening.

JARROD
What is happening that I should know about?

GRAFFOR
Otthuilku and Rajaooku have entered Vancouver and are fighting each other in the city.

                    JARROD
          I'll be there.

Jarrod hangs up.

Joseph continues talking on his phone.

                    JOSEPH
          I'm on my way.

Joseph hangs up and turns to Jarrod.

                    JOSEPH (CONT'D)
          I take it you received a similar
          call to mine.

                    JARROD
          The monsters are here and we're
          needed at the lab.

Claire stares at Jarrod. He kisses her and kisses his son on the forehead.

                    JARROD (CONT'D)
          We'll be back, honey.

                    CLAIRE
          I know.

                    JOSEPH
          Nice seeing you again, Claire and
          Elias.

                    CLAIRE
          Same here, Mr. Crowe.

The door closes. Claire rubs Elias' hair.

EXT. VANCOUVER, BRITISH COLUMBIA, CANADA - CONTINUOUS

The city is nearly covered in complete flames as Otthuilku and Rajaooku battle it out in the city. Otthuilku continues swiping its tail in the air, trying to make contact with Rajaooku. Rajaooku shrieks as it swoops down and collides with Otthuilku, knocking it to the ground, through the buildings close by. Rajaooku flies in the air and dives down on Otthuilku's abdomen. Otthuilku roars in pain as Rajaooku is beating down on it. Rajaooku hovers into the air and starts to circle Otthuilku as it gets up to its feet. Rajaooku causes a small tornado to appear and grab Otthuilku, tossing it into one of the larger buildings.

Rajaooku shrieks as its defeating Otthuilku.

INT. LAB - CONTINUOUS

Jarrod and Joseph arrive at the lab. Seeing Graffor and Deborah watching the battle unfold from a safe distance.

                    GRAFFOR
    Glad to see you made it.

                    JARROD
    Same goes to you two.

                    JOSEPH
    What's going on with the monsters?

                    GRAFFOR
    They're having it out. The battle
    that will end not only this event,
    but could have a hand in ending the
    world we know.

Jarrod looks at Graffor. Concerned to an extent.

                    JOSEPH
    What do you mean?

Deborah hands Graffor a bible and he places it on the nearby table. He also has the Book of Enoch, Book of Jasher, and Book of Jubilees laying on the table next to the Bible.

                    GRAFFOR
    The end it speaks of is currently
    taking form right out there.

                    JOSEPH
    You mean the apocalypse.

                    JARROD
    The three beasts mirror
    Revelation's three symbolic beasts
    as well do they mirror the three
    beasts created by Yahweh. It makes
    sense now.

                    JOSEPH
    From what you're saying, only God
    can defeat these beasts? That's
    what your saying?

                    JARROD
    Yeah.

Joseph scratches his head.

                    JOSEPH
          So, what can we do now about all of
          this?

The room is silent, only the sound of the battle can be
heard.

                    JOSEPH (CONT'D)
          Well?!

                    GRAFFOR
          We can only wait and see what the
          outcome will be of this battle.
          Then, will we know what truly
          awaits us.

Graffor watches the battle from the outside patio of the
laboratory.

EXT. VANCOUVER, BRITISH COLUMBIA, CANADA - CONTINUOUS

Rajaooku continues beating down Otthuilku and even grabs
pieces of destroyed buildings and starts dropping them onto
Otthuilku. Rajaooku shrieks, glorifying itself in the battle,
believing it has the fight won.

Rajaooku shrieks until a rumbling sound occurs. The area
begins to flash a gold-like color. The rumbilng increases and
turns into a humming sound. The clouds become darker as the
fire have enlarged themselves. In the clouds we can see the
golden light shines. Lightning strikes and its Otthuilku,
back on its feet with the golden light shining from its eyes
and spine. Otthuilku faces Rajaooku and inhales slowly.
Then.....

A ray of golden-red energy releases from Otthuilku's mouth.
Otthuilku's eyes shining in gold as the energy begins to
consume Rajaooku from its position, burning its feathered
flesh.

EXT. LAB PATIO - CONTINUOUS

Graffor watches Otthuiku releasing the energy on Rajaooku.
Joseph sees it and points. Jarrod watches.

                    JOSEPH
          Did you see that?

                    JARROD
          Yeah. Its a shocker.

GRAFFOR
Its a simple understanding. The ancients had a name for something like that.

Joseph looks at Graffor.

JOSEPH
What did they call it?

GRAFFOR
The Purging of *Yah*.

They continue to watch.

EXT. VANCOUVER, BRITISH COLUMBIA, CANADA - CONTINUOUS

Otthuilku releases another blast of the energy, burning Rajaooku as it shrieks in pain. Rajaooku crashes into one of the buildings and fall to the ground. Otthuilku walks over to the flying creature and begins stomping on its body.

From the distance, we see an array of military helicopters approaching. The lay on top of the nearest buildings they can see that were far enough from the battle.

Soldiers gather on the rooftops of the buildings. Weapons in hand. They stand as they're awaiting the order to fire at the monsters.

EXT. ROOFTOP - CONTINUOUS

The Commanding Soldier leads the other soldiers to their positions.

COMMANDING SOLDIER
We stay in our positions until the signal is given for us to attack!

The soldiers all shout, "Yes sir."

EXT. VANCOUVER, BRITISH COLUMBIA, CANADA - CONTINUOUS

Otthuilku continues stomping Rajaooku into the ground, causing a small crater to form underneath its body. As Otthuilku's foot comes down toward Rajaooku's head, it moves its head from the stomp and dives its beak into Otthuilku's leg. Otthuilku roars in pain as Rajaooku is free from the secluded area and flies into the sky.

Otthuilku tries to reach Rajaooku in the air, but fails to do so. Otthuilku stands still, crouching over. Its back begins to take shape.

EXT. LAB PATIO - CONTINUOUS

They continue to watch the battle take place. Jarrod sees Otthuilku crouched over.

JARROD
What is Otthuilku doing?

GRAFFOR
I do not know.

EXT. VANCOUVER, BRITISH COLUMBIA, CANADA - CONTINUOUS

Otthuilku is crouched over as its back continues changing and forming. Rajaooku hovers in the sky watching Otthuilku. Rajaooku shrieks as Otthuilku raises up, standing upright. The thunder roars as Otthuilku stares at Rajaooku when lightning bolts strike Otthuilku and from its back, two long dragon-like wings shoot out, showing their long wingspan. Rajaooku even startles at the sight.

EXT. ROOFTOP - CONTINUOUS

The soldiers witness the wings of Otthuilku being revealed.

SOLDIER
Oh shit. You seen that?!

COMMANDING SOLDIER
Yeah.

EXT. LAB PATIO - CONTINUOUS

Joseph covers his mouth from the surprising reveal.

JOSEPH
It has wings.

GRAFFOR
This is an intriguing discovery.

JARROD
I didn't know it had any wings.

                    GRAFFOR
          The Leviathan does not have any
          wings. I believe something is
          taking place that we have just
          begun to learn.

They watch as the wings of Otthuilku stretch out. Facing Rajaooku.

EXT. VANCOUVER, BRITISH COLUMBIA, CANADA - CONTINUOUS

Rajaooku shrieks as it flies off. Otthuilku jumps up and flies off behind Rajaooku, chasing it down in the air.

EXT. SKY - CONTINUOUS

Otthuilku and Rajaooku fly through the air as Otthuilku chases Rajaooku down. Rajaooku swoops and twists as it flies in the air. Rajaooku dives down through the clouds, so does Otthuilku as lightning strikes its body.

EXT. VANCOUVER, BRITISH COLUMBIA, CANADA - CONTINUOUS

Otthuilku and Rajaooku dive down from the clouds over the city. The city looks as if its been turning into an earthly hell with fire all throughout the city. Rajaooku twists and flies over the rooftops where the soldiers were present. Otthuilku flies through from behind.

Otthuilku roars as it releases another blast of energy from behind, hitting Rajaooku in its back, casing the beast to collapse onto the ground, ramming through buildings in its path. Otthuilku lands as its wings fold into its back. Otthuilu walks over toward Rajaooku, who's down on the ground and covered in rubble from the buildings.

Otthuilku roars at Rajaooku, until Rajaooku jumps up and blows a large gust of wind toward Otthuilku, knocking it down. Rajaooku hovers into the air and lands on a nearby building. Shrieking of its current stance. Otthuilku stands up and roars. Rajaooku flies toward Otthuilku and as Rajaooku gets closer, Otthuilku turns and swipes its tail into Rajaooku, right into a building. The building collapses with Rajaooku caught in its grasp.

The building falls as Rajaooku falls to the ground with it.

EXT. LAB PATIO - CONTINUOUS

Continuing watching the battle, Graffor looks toward the fight. Jarrod approaches Graffor.

> JARROD
> What do you think will happen after this bout is over?

> GRAFFOR
> I believe that the victor will return to its previous state. But, things to tend to change on earth do they.

Jarrod nods as Graffor returns inside the lab. Jarrod looks on at the battle.

EXT. ROOFTOP - CONTINUOUS

The soldiers still wait in position.

> SOLDIER
> How long do we wait here doing absolutely nothing?

> COMMANDING SOLDIER
> We wait for the signal and then we fire at the monsters.

The soldier sighs.

> SOLDIER
> We have the bitches in our hands. Let's just take our shots from here and call it a night.

> COMMANDING SOLDIER
> We do the orders that we given to us. We wait until the signal.

> SOLDIER
> What if the signal doesn't show up at the right time?

The Commanding Soldier stands up from his position and faces the other soldier. Eyes locked on one another.

> COMMANDING SOLDIER
> We fire when commanded. That's an order. Keep it in your thick skull, soldier.

The soldier nods arrogantly. The Commanding Soldier returns to his position, targeted at Otthuilku and Rajaooku in the distance of the buildings.

                    SOLDIER
     Alright, man.

The soldier points his machine gun toward Otthuilku and begins firing. Catching the other soldiers completely off guard. The other soldier rams the soldier to the ground.

                COMMANDING SOLDIER
     The hell are you doing, boy?!

                    SOLDIER
     Get off of me! We have our
     opportunity to fire at the bastards
     now!

The shots attract Otthuilku to their location. The soldiers look and see Otthuilku coming toward them in the distance. The soldier looks down at the soldier on the ground.

                COMMANDING SOLDIER
     I am beyond the measuring stick of
     kicking your ass and handing you
     over to the monsters. You just
     ruined this whole operation.

The Commanding Soldier leaves the other soldier on the ground, who gets to his feet and begins firing at Otthuilku along with the other soldiers on the rooftops. Otthuilku roars as it approaches the buildings.

From behind, Rajaooku rises up and swoops over toward Otthuilku, ramming into the back of Otthuilku's head, Rajaooku causes Otthuilku to crash into one of the buildings, bringing it down and the soldiers that were stained on top as well. Otthuilku falls onto the rubble as Rajaooku flies and rams the other buildings with the soldiers on top.

                    SOLDIER
     Oh shit! They're taking us out
     building by building!

                COMMANDING SOLDIER
     This is all your fault, you little
     shit!

The soldier runs over and punches the soldier. He falls to the ground, holding his mouth. The Commanding Soldier takes the machine gun away from the soldier.

                    COMMANDING SOLDIER (CONT'D)
               You better get your shit together.

The Commanding Soldier walks away and fires at Rajaooku,
flying toward his location. Rajaooku shrieks as it flies over
the rooftop and fans its wing, blowing many of the soldiers
and their helicopters from the top of the building. Some of
the soldiers hold on to the edge of the rooftop.

                    COMMANDING SOLDIER (CONT'D)
               Take my hand, soldier! Just reach!

The soldier tries to reach, but feels himself slipping from
his current spot. He extends his hand out toward the
Commanding Soldier.

                    SOLDIER
               I can't reach any further,
               Commander!

                    COMMANDING SOLDIER
               Come on! You can reach! Keep coming
               closer!

                    SOLDIER
               I can't!

Rajaooku flies toward them as it snatches the soldier from
the edge and shakes him around in its mouth before swallowing
the soldier's body whole.

The Commanding Soldier sits in terror as he watches Rajaooku
fly through the air after killing and swallowing one of his
recruited soldiers. He grabs his gun.

                    COMMANDING SOLDIER
          No.

The Commanding Soldier begins firing at Rajaooku as Otthuilku
rises up from the debris and turns around, causing its tail
to collide with the other buildings and takes them down along
with the remaining soldiers. The Commanding Soldier falls to
his death still firing the gun at both monsters until he hits
the rubble.

EXT. LAB PATIO - CONTINUOUS

They witness the buildings falling and can see and hear the
gunshots being fired from the soldiers.

                    JARROD
               Those soldiers were on top of those
               buildings.

JOSEPH
Who authorize more troops to be sent over here?

GRAFFOR
It had to be Admiral. I believe he wanted to keep a secure area protected so his men could go in and take out the beasts themselves.

JOSEPH
But, you've already said that only God can be the one to kill them?

Jarrod glances over at Joseph.

JARROD
I sense a change in you. Are you slowly getting the understanding?

JOSEPH
This event is starting to wake me up about a lot of things.

GRAFFOR
Don't get too carried away with it. For some much knowledge will make you go mad.

JOSEPH
True. You have a point.

Jarrod smirks.

JOSEPH (CONT'D)
I noticed there weren't any news choppers flying around out there.

GRAFFOR
Rajaooku would've flown straight through them and they wouldn't even stand a chance much less get a recording for their story.

Joseph nods.

EXT. VANCOUVER, BRITISH COLUMBIA, CANADA - CONTINUOUS

Otthuilku and Rajaooku continue to fight one another through various means of tail swiping, claw swiping, and biting. Rajaooku flies overhead of Otthuilku and bites the back of its neck. Otthuilku roars as it attempts to shake Rajaooku from its back.

Rajaooku releases the hood as Otthuilku swipes its arm back, hitting Rajaooku in its head. Rajaooku falls to the ground as Otthuilku starts stomping the creature. Otthuilku places its foot on the chest of Rajaooku. Otthuilku breathes in and releases another blasts of energy, pointing directly at the head of Rajaooku. Rajaooku shrieks in pain as the energy is not only burning, but melting its flesh. Otthuilku increases the blast until the head or Rajaooku is completely melted and nothing but burnt feathered flesh and bone.

Otthuilku takes a step back and roars in its victory.

EXT. LAB PATIO - CONTINUOUS

Graffor looks on in complete awe.

> GRAFFOR
> Rajaooku is dead. Otthuilku is the victor.

Jarrod, Joseph, and Deborah watch on as they see Otthuilku roaring in victory.

EXT. VANCOUVER, BRITISH COLUMBIA, CANADA - CONTINUOUS

Otthuilku finishes roaring as it looks down at the dead body of Rajaooku. Otthuilku crouches down and grabs the melted head of Rajaooku and drops it to the ground. Otthuilku looks around before its wings shoot from its back and it flies into the air, through the thick clouds.

People that survived the battle in the city started to come out of the buildings, looking around and looking up toward the sky, seeing Otthuilku's silhouette in the clouds. People point up toward the clouds.

Otthuilku comes back down from the clouds and lands in the midst of the destruction.

A news helicopter arrives at the scene, showcasing Otthuilku as the victor of the grueling battle against Rajaooku. The headline of the live story is titled, **"The Eleventh Hour at hand?"**

INT. MILITARY BASE - CONTINUOUS

Admiral Meryl and Colonel Smith watch the news feed from the base. Admiral sits down at the table, releasing a sigh of relief.

ADMIRAL MERYL
It seems that this event is over
and we can continue to our previous
duties.

COLONEL SMITH
Will do just that, Admiral.

Colonel Smith leaves the room, leaving Admiral to sit as he watches the news feed of Otthuilku's victory.

INT. JARROD'S HOME - CONTINUOUS

Claire watches the news feed from her laptop. Elias, sitting in a chair next to her can also see the feed.

ELIAS
Mommy, will the monster be here
tomorrow?

Claire looks at her son.

CLAIRE
I do not know, Elias.

INT. JOSEPH'S HOME - CONTINUOUS

Sandra watches the news in the living room of the house. She stares as it shows Otthuilku on the screen. She shakes her head.

SANDRA
What do you know.

EXT. LAB PATIO - CONTINUOUS

Graffor watches on. Jarrod, Joseph, and Deborah do the same.

DEBORAH
What do you think he will do next,
Doctor?

GRAFFOR
I have no idea, but I intend on
finding out.

Deborah smiles as she returns to inside the lab. Jarrod stares on.

                    JARROD
          So, how will this all play out in
          the future for certain?

                    GRAFFOR
          We'll have to wait and find out.
          Don't want to get ahead ourselves.

Jarrod smiles.

                    JOSEPH
          If you don't mind, I would love to
          learn more about this. This kind of
          stuff is what keeps guys like us
          going. Unraveling mysteries like
          these. What an opportunity to be
          had.

Graffor approaches Joseph.

                    GRAFFOR
          I sincerely hope you are prepared
          for what comes in the aftermath of
          this whole thing. Because, if
          you're not then you might not be
          ready for the next event.

A beat.

Joseph pauses. Thinking to himself.

                    JOSEPH
          What next event?

                    GRAFFOR
          It doesn't need to be said, Dr.
          Crowe. It will be seen my everyone
          around the world at one time.

Joseph looks toward Jarrod. Pointing at Graffor.

                    JOSEPH
          What is he talking about, Jarrod?
          Is it this important that I must
          know about it?

                    JARROD
          I have a clue to what he is talking
          about. But, we can discuss it
          tomorrow. I think we've had
          ourselves enough for a day.

Joseph shrugs.

                    JOSEPH
          I can agree. Tomorrow then.

                    JARROD
          Tomorrow it is.

EXT. VANCOUVER, BRITISH COLUMBIA, CANADA - CONTINUOUS

Otthuilku walks away from the destroyed city toward the bay.
Otthuilku gives off one more roar before diving into the bay
and swimming off into the sea. Vanishing back into legend.

SUBTITLE: THREE YEARS LATER.

INT. CONFERENCE ROOM - DAY

Joseph stands at a podium in a conference room with many
scientists and historians sitting down. Joseph has a
powerpoint behind him, showing an historic drawing of the
three monsters, Otthuilku, Meheooku, and Rajaooku.

                    JOSEPH
          It has seemed to be that these
          monsters that we once thought of as
          myth, are real. They exist among us
          and we must do our due diligence in
          order to learn and to be prepared
          for anything to come that will be
          similar to the event that took
          place a year ago.

Graffor walks into the room behind Joseph and stands next to
him by the powerpoint board.

                    JOSEPH (CONT'D)
          Dr. Schewaz Graffor has come to
          give full detail of my
          investigation of these creatures
          and their legendary backgrounds.

Graffor shakes Joseph's hand. Taking over the conference
room. Graffor grabs a microphone, looking out to the audience
in the room.

                    GRAFFOR
          I am aware that many of you have a
          lot of intriguing and interesting
          questions about the three monsters.
          I call them, "chevah", which means
          beast in Hebrew.
                         (MORE)

GRAFFOR (CONT'D)
Now, these chevah are more than likely a symbolic reference to the Book of Revelation. Where the three beasts appeared from echo the same locations that are talked about in Revelation. Simply put, Otthuilku, the Leviathan came from the sea. Meheooku, the Behemoth came from underneath the ground, and Rajaooku, the Zoz came from the sky.

INT. JARROD'S LAND - DAY

Jarrod is seen working on a building project with others that live on the land. From the door of Jarrod's home comes Elias, now ten years old, comes running out of the house toward Jarrod and the other guys.

ELIAS
Can I help out with the building, father?

JARROD
Yeah. You could be a great helping hand.

Elias smiles as he listens to the directions Jarrod gives him along with the other guys working on the building.

Claire steps out from the doorway, pregnant with another child. She smiles as she watches Elias learn from his father.

INT. CONFERENCE ROOM - CONTINUOUS

GRAFFOR
The event that occurred three years ago is only a small sample of what will and shall occur in years time or it could happen this year at the exact same time as the first event.

Joseph stands by the door with Sandra at his side. They listen to Graffor speak with the audience.

GRAFFOR (CONT'D)
Sure, this all might sound like some fairy tale fantasy that was passed down the generations.
(MORE)

                    GRAFFOR (CONT'D)
          But, we already know that there is
          something taking shape in the
          universe and it will ultimately
          climax here on Earth.

EXT. HISTORY EXHIBIT - CONTINUOUS

We see hundreds of people walking through an exhibit of
historical artifacts. The people walk through and pause at
one area of the exhibit. The exhibition they are looking at
is a particle of the melted head of Rajaooku. The people take
photos of the particle. Excited and thrilled to be close to
the object that was once part of a living creature.

                    GRAFFOR
               (O.S.)
          *I can also understand that many
          people were not prepared for an
          event like this and are surely not
          thinking about preparing for
          another one when it occurs.*

Some of the people are dressed up in costumes of Otthuilku,
Meheooku, and Rajaooku. Mocking the battle between the
monsters and acting it out amongst large crowds.

INT. CONFERENCE ROOM - CONTINUOUS

One man raises his hand up. Vigorously to ask a question.
Graffor points toward him.

                    GRAFFOR
          Yes.

                    HISTORIAN
          I remember specifically hearing
          about how God is the only one to be
          able to kill the three monsters and
          yet Otthuilku killed two of them.
          Would you like the comment on that
          theory?

                    GRAFFOR
          I would be delighted to comment.

The scientists and historians prepare themselves for the
answer of the question. So does Graffor, as he believes they
are not yet ready for the answer to be given out.

                    GRAFFOR (CONT'D)
          I also said and it is also known in
          history.

INT. MILITARY BASE - CONTINUOUS

Admiral Meryl trains the up and coming soldiers with Colonel
Smith by his side.

The soldiers are doing exercises, preparing for the training
ahead.

                    GRAFFOR
                (O.S.)
          *That only Yahweh the Elohim is the
          only one to have the power to kill
          any of the three beasts and two of
          them are dead.*

INT. CONFERENCE ROOM - CONTINUOUS

Graffor pauses and faces the audience in front of him. He
smiles.

                    GRAFFOR
          So, that leaves me and you with one
          question to ask ourselves of that
          particular matter.

EXT. SEA - CONTINUOUS

The sea is calm. The sun shines down upon it. Glistening the
water.

                    GRAFFOR
                (O.S.)
          *Who was really in control of this
          event? Who released the monsters
          from their secured habitat? Who
          directed their paths? More so, who
          decided which chevah would live and
          which chevah would die?*

The sea starts to shake as waves slowly grow out of its
depths.

                    GRAFFOR (CONT'D)
               (O.S.)
          I thoroughly believe that the
          Leviathan, Otthuilku didn't come to
          avert the apocalypse.

The waves intensify. Clouds cover the sky, bringing darkness to the sea as the water grow impatient. Thunder roars from the heavens.

                    GRAFFOR (CONT'D)
               (O.S.)
          I believe it came to fulfill it.

Thunder continues to roar as lightning strikes the sea. Rain begins to pour down hard upon the sea waters as the tail of Otthuilku rises from the ocean. A low thump is heard.

CUT TO BLACK

And I heard a great voice out of the temple saying to the seven angels, Go your ways, and pour out the vials of the wrath of Yahweh your Elohim upon the earth. - Revelation 16:1

(CONT'D)

CREDITS

END.

ENTER THE UNIVERSE OF REALMS

ABOUT THE AUTHOR

Ty'Ron W. C. Robinson II is the author of several works of fiction. Including the *Dark Titan Universe Saga* series (*Dark Titan Knights, The Resistance Protocol, Tales of the Scattered, Tales of the Numinous, Day of Octagon, Crossbreed, Heaven's Called*), *The Haunted City Saga* series, the *Symbolum Venatores* series, and the *Frightened!* series.

Also of other books (*Lost in Shadows, The Book of The Elect, etc.*) and One-Shot short stories.

More information pertaining to the author and stories can be found at darktitanentertainment.com.

Twitter: @TyRonRobinsonII
Vero: @tyronrobinsonii

Twitter: @DarkTitan_
Instagram: @darktitanentertainment
Facebook: @DarkTitanEnt

www.ingramcontent.com/pod-product-compliance
Lightning Source LLC
Chambersburg PA
CBHW080036120526
44589CB00036B/2555